Towards a More Coherent Global Economic Order

Publisher's Note

The books published in the *Forward Studies Series* contain a selection of research studies, reports, seminar or conference proceedings of the European Commission's Forward Studies Unit.

In publishing these works in the *Forward Studies Series*, the original material has undergone editorial rearrangement. Bibliographies have been added where necessary.

Forward Studies Series

TOWARDS A MORE COHERENT GLOBAL ECONOMIC ORDER

Foreword by Jacques Santer

St. Martin's Press
New York

Office for Official Publications
of the European Communities

337
T737

TOWARDS A MORE COHERENT GLOBAL ECONOMIC ORDER

St. Martin's Press, Scholarly and Reference Division,
175 Fifth Avenue, New York, N.Y. 10010

First published in the United States of America in 1998

Printed in Great Britain

ISBN: 0-312-21602-5

Library of Congress Cataloging-in-Publication Data

Towards a more coherent global economic order / Forward Studies Unit
   at the European Commission.
      p.   cm.
   Based on: Report on Global economic order.
   Includes bibliographical references.
   ISBN 0-312-21602-5 (cloth)
      1. International economic relations. 2. International trade.
3. Commercial policy. 4. Economic stabilization. 5. European Union
countries–Commercial Policy. I. European Commission. Forward Studies
Unit. II. Report on global economic order.
HF 1359.T69   1998
337–DC21   98–17449
                                                               CIP

Contents

Foreword

I am pleased to see that what was originally published as the *Report on Global Economic Order* is being made available to the public as a book in the *Forward Studies Series*.

The publication draws on the expertise of different services in the European Commission to present the case for institutional change in international economic relations.

The case is based on a broad analysis of the key changes in the world economy. The proposals for institutional change range from adjustments to current arrangements to the creation of new structures. The objective is the same: to restore coherence between the changed world economy and newly recognized goals of international action on the one hand, and the institutional set-up at international level, largely inherited from the aftermath of World War II, on the other hand.

The reading of the publication leads me to stress two types of conclusions: one in terms of general analysis, the other in terms of practical reform options.

If one looks at the way the world economy has evolved since the end of World War II, and in more recent years in particular, the need for change in the regulatory framework of international economic relations becomes evident. Three major developments call for a revision of international institutions:

1. globalization, bringing into the international arena issues and policies traditionally regarded as purely domestic;
2. the changing balance of economic power, with the rapid emergence of new economic powerhouses;
3. the end of the Cold War, with the implicit decoupling of political from economic alignments.

At the same level of importance, one should regard the growing awareness that international economic order is not only about trade and growth, but that environmental and social sustainability are also increasingly at stake on a world basis.

In terms of practical reforms, one can in turn detect two main lines of action:

- 'strengthening the pillars': reforms to ensure that certain areas, the importance of which has grown with time, are better covered at international level. The establishment of the World Trade Organization, as a successor to the General Agreement on Tariffs and Trade, but with a greatly expanded remit and power, is a development of the greatest importance. Much remains to be done, however, for example in dealing with environmental problems which are global in scope;
- 'strengthening the interfaces': reforms to improve coordination between international institutions and to facilitate the handling of interdependencies between areas. There is a general agreement that international institutions should avoid acting at cross-purposes and efforts should be made to take into account the broad picture, particularly when it comes to issues of development. The current debate on the reform of the United Nations in the economic and social areas revolves largely around these problems. The proposals tabled by the European Union, concerning in particular the strengthening of the role of the UN Secretariat and the ECOSOC, represent a good illustration of the type of reform advocated in the Report. The Report, however, also advocates bolder steps in the direction of an overarching structure to ensure coherence in the economic sphere.

Finally, I would like to emphasize a conclusion which relates more directly to the European experience. As the Report makes clear, the European Union has much to offer in the way of shaping a more coherent world order. This not only on account of its weight in the world economic arena, but also because of its unique experience: the problems of interdependence that the world is encountering today have long been taken into account in Europe, which has progressed more than anywhere else in the exercise of supra-national decision making. But for the world to draw the full benefit from the European experience, Europe must be able to speak with a single voice. This is a challenge which the European Union addresses in its own reform process, formally undertaken in the Amsterdam Treaty.

Jacques Santer
President of the
European Commission

Preface

The 50th anniversary of the United Nations and the Bretton Woods institutions and the 1994 G–7 Naples Summit decision to conduct a review of these institutions prompted the launch of a study project within the Commission on the set of principles, rules and decision-making procedures known as the 'international economic order' and its relation to a changing world. This reflection has resulted in the production of the *Report on Global Economic Order*, on which this book is based.

The Report did not necessarily reflect the views of all the services involved in its preparation. It is a contribution to the reflection issued under the sole responsibility of the leaders of the project.

The Report was completed under the guidance of Joly Dixon, Director for international economic and financial matters in the Directorate-General for Economic and Financial Affairs, and Jérôme Vignon, Principal Adviser in the Forward Studies Unit.

The completion of the Report was entrusted to a task force including Christoph Bail and Lucio R. Pench (Forward Studies Unit), Michael Neilson and Elena Flores Gual (Directorate-General for Economic and Financial Affairs), Bernard Brunet and Roy Dickinson (Directorate-General for External Relations: Commercial Policy and Relations with North America, the Far East, Australia and New Zealand). The final revision of the report was undertaken by L.R. Pench.

The task force benefited from the preparatory work undertaken by an informal interservice group on international economic order.

Helpful assistance in the preparation of the final text was given by Sylvie Barès and Fabienne Barbier (Forward Studies Unit).

Joly Dixon   *Jérôme Vignon*

List of abbreviations

APEC	Asia Pacific Economic Co-operation
ASEAN	Association of South-East Asian Nations
BIS	Bank for International Settlements
CITES	Convention on International Trade in Endangered Species of Wild Flora and Fauna
CSD	Commission on Sustainable Development
ECOSOC	Economic and Social Council (UN)
EMU	Economic and Monetary Union
EU	European Union
FDI	foreign direct investment
FSU	Former Soviet Union
GATS	General Agreement on Trade in Services
GATT	General Agreement on Tariffs and Trade
GEF	Global Environment Fund
GNP	Gross national product
IDA	International Development Association
IFI	International financial institution
IGC	Intergovernmental Conference
ILO	International Labour Organization
IMF	International Monetary Fund
LDC	least developed countries
MEA	Multilateral Environmental Agreements
MERCOSUR	Mercado Común del Sur (South American regional organization)
MFA	Multi-Fibre Arrangement
MFN	most favoured nation
NAFTA	North American Free Trade Agreement
ODA	official development aid

OECD	Organization for Economic Co-operation and Development
OMA	Orderly marketing agreements
QR	quantitative restriction
R&D	research and development
TRIMs	trade related investment measures (General Agreement on Trade in Services – GATS)
TRIPs	trade related intellectual property rights (General Agreement on Trade in Services – GATS)
UN	United Nations
UNCED	United Nations Conference on Environment and Development
UNCTAD	United Nations Conference on Trade and Development
UNDP	United Nations Development Programme
UNEP	United Nations Environment Programme
VER	voluntary export restraint
WB	World Bank
WTO	World Trade Organization

Background and purpose

The objective of the Report was to examine the functioning of the system as a whole, and the extent to which change is needed. It deals with the international economic order, broadly defined, but *not* with wider linkages (e.g. collective security, international crime). The main focus is on long-term trends in the international economy, and thus on the long-term directions of institutional change.

The approach taken has been to look at problems with current arrangements, arising notably from major international political realignments and shifts in the balance of economic power and the trend toward globalization of markets, then to consider institutional solutions. Looking at the system as a whole has meant concentrating on interactions between policy areas (though major problems within policy areas have also been treated). Since it is not possible to deal with all interactions, a limited number of issue-areas or 'clusters' have been identified.

This approach should allow an examination of three inter-related questions:

- Are changes needed within particular policy areas and institutions?
- Are changes needed in the way institutions coordinate to take account of interactions between policy areas?
- Is more than improved cooperation needed? Is there a case for further institutional development?

The Halifax 1995 G-7 Summit followed up the institutional review process by producing a number of policy recommendations and institutional indications. However, these indications and recommendations were relatively limited in scope and time horizon, while the nature of the problems suggests a systemic and long-term approach. By contrast, the present document aims at focusing the reflection on the more fundamental issues in the international economic order in a comprehensive and longer-term perspective, one in which more important changes in the institutional set-up can be contemplated. It does so by developing an general framework of analysis, trying to apply it to a number of domains and finally drawing conclusions for the system as a whole. In doing so it should help the Commission in the task of ensuring an overall consistency in the overall posture of the EU in international economic relations.

Introduction and summary

The Report on which this book is based is an evaluation of the potential for reform of the institutions of the international economic order undertaken on the occasion of the 50th anniversary of the United Nations and the Bretton Woods institutions and the institutional review launched at the Naples 1994 G-7 Summit.

The Report focused on long-term trends in the international economy and the requirements of institutional change. This includes a consideration of the European Union's place in the international economic order.

Key changes taking place in the world economy are:

- the globalization of markets, driven by progress in transportation and communication technology, liberalization of trade and investment and changes in enterprise organization and strategy, and resulting in:
  - growing interdependence of national economies, with some national policy instruments (e.g., fiscal and monetary policies) becoming less effective and some domestic policies (e.g. competition policies, industrial, social and environmental standards) increasingly taking on an international dimension because of their impact on the conditions of international competition;
  - growing interaction between policy areas at international level, with policy decisions in one area having increasing effects in other areas (e.g. trade, environment and development);
- the changing balance of economic power, illustrated by the

rapid emergence of new economic powerhouses, particularly in Asia;
- the end of the Cold War, with the pursuit of economic interests being less constrained by security considerations and North–South relations being decoupled from political alignments.

At the same time, there has been a shift in the objectives that the international economic order must address, from a relatively narrow focus on growth and preservation of trade, to the more complex goal of sustainable development, which means integrating economic efficiency, macroeconomic stability, social justice and environmental sustainability.

The main concern emerging from the Report is about a growing mismatch between, on the one hand, the changes in the world economy and in the overall goal of international action and, on the other hand, the existing institutional set up at international level.

The institutions of the international economic order, essentially dating back to the conclusion of World War II, have served the world well in promoting economic integration and have proved remarkably flexible in adapting to changing economic circumstances. However, important gaps remain in some areas and in dealing with the interactions between areas; moreover, the functional institutions' policy autonomy restricts their capacity to cope fully with the challenge of complexity, both in terms of interactions and objectives. There is a growing need for a more coherent framework: for more intense and effective coordination of policies; regimes better adapted to promoting sustainable economic, social and environmental development while going with the grain of the markets; and, in some cases, for genuine supranational decision-making.

The European Union must play a role corresponding to its weight in the world economy if adequate progress is to be made in resolving this mismatch, demonstrating that the narrow pursuit of national interests is self-defeating in an increasingly interdependent world. It is among the main powers' responsibilities and in their ultimate interest to pay special attention to the international consequences of their actions so as to preserve and strengthen the international order. A more effective and enhanced role for the European Union would also be a powerful means of countering pressure towards protectionism in individual states and the temptation of 'fortress Europe'.

The rest of the executive summary draws out the main policy issues and conclusions of the work, but does not seek to summarize the entire contents of the Report.

APPROACHING REFORM OF THE INTERNATIONAL ECONOMIC ORDER

Before assessing specific areas or institutional issues the Report looks at the functioning of the post-war international economic order, and at approaches to dealing with interdependence.

The international economic order is made up of a wide variety of arrangements involving different degrees of intensity of cooperation. These can be characterized on a continuum between 'shallow' integration (removing barriers 'at the border' and their equivalents without attempt to bring national regulations and practices into line) and 'deep integration' (liberalization accompanied by coordination/harmonization of domestic regulatory policies or some genuine supra-national decision-making).

Broadly speaking, the international order remains near to the shallow integration end of the spectrum. The European single market is probably the most important case of deep integration. National differences in interests and preferences and in the perception of the need for collective action will continue to condition the degree of policy integration. This means that diversity of approaches to suit national circumstances will remain in most cases appropriate. Any move towards deep integration should only take place where national action, or simple intergovernmental cooperation, cannot adequately cope with problems raised by globalization (principle of 'global subsidiarity').

But the provision of mechanisms to ensure systemic stability, dealing with spillovers such as arise with the environment, and the pursuit of the objective of justice in international relations show the importance of considering the case for enhanced international coordination in a range of areas.

The substance of the Report therefore concerned those issue-areas where the adequacy of the shallow integration approach can be questioned.

Behind the analyses and the conclusions of the Report lies substantial background work, drawing on the expertise of different services in the Commission, aimed at identifying the main problems. Having identified what appeared to be the most important and problematic interactions (the 'clusters') around the different 'building blocks' of the international economic order (trade, development, the environment, finance and macroeconomics), ways of dealing with these problems have been sought, focusing on the 'pillars' (the key functional institutions and regimes) and, even more, on the 'interfaces' (cooperation/coordination between pillars). This corresponds to an 'issues first, institutions after' approach, where ideas for institutional reform are supported by evidence that current arrangements are not working adequately.

KEY POLICY PROBLEMS AND WAYS FORWARD IN SPECIFIC ISSUE-AREAS

The analysis of the problems related to the four issue-areas or 'clusters' selected for consideration points to the need both to reinforce some pillars of the international order, and to deal better with interactions between pillars. In terms of key policy problems and recommendations, this means the following:

For 'new' areas and traditionally 'domestic' areas and their links to trade

The progress of globalization, of which trade and investment liberalization is an essential driver, means that previously ignored or domestically treated policy areas (e.g. environment, competition, labour standards, technical standards not least for the information society) are perceived as having an increasing impact on the conditions of international competition, and hence increasingly become trade-related. If 'rules of the game' at international level in these areas are not developed, the risk is that quick-fix solutions involving trade policy instruments will be resorted to, leading to an unravelling of the liberal regime for trade and investment that has underpinned prosperity after World War II. Priorities in this issue-area include:

- establish strong and effective international regimes, not least in order to head off protectionist pressures. First priorities should include investment and competition. For investment, it must be ensured that negotiations in the OECD are rapidly supplemented by a similar effort in the WTO. As regards competition, a plurilateral agreement among regulatory authorities might address some of the most pressing issues and pave the way for a global agreement that could be integrated into the WTO. In both areas, strong leadership from the European Union and in particular of the Commission in the years ahead will be crucial if these goals are to be met;
- make the WTO one of the key pillars of the international economic order. Its membership should become truly universal and its resources commensurate with its responsibilities. It should develop criteria to help ensure compatibility between rules in new policy areas and the trade regime (notably in terms of criteria restricting use of trade policy instruments to enforce these new rules). An important step

5

in this direction would be amending the GATT (Art. XX) to make WTO rules and Multilateral Environmental Agreements (MEAs) mutually compatible. Any linkage between trade and labour standards should be conditioned to consensus at ILO level on definition and monitoring of basic rights of people at work;

- set up effective collaboration between the WTO, on the one hand, and the IFIs (and the UN agencies), on the other hand. This will help address the interactions between trade policy and other policy areas, while preserving the value of the WTO as a forum for facilitating and liberalizing trade.

For development and its links with macroeconomic stabilization, trade, the environment and migration policies

The exclusion of a large number of countries from the benefits of integration in the international economy is a major failure of the economic order. Some of the obstacles to integration are the responsibility of the international community (e.g. unstable macroeconomic environment, barriers to market access, insufficient volume and distorted distribution of aid flows); other obstacles are mainly created by the developing countries themselves (e.g. ideologically driven mis-development, lack of democratic participation and discrimination against women and minorities). A common problem cutting across development policy failures is that some of the key levers (e.g. trade access, macroeconomic stability) are outside the traditional scope of 'development' policy. Priorities in this issue-area are:

- integrate more systematically the development dimension in all other policy areas, notably trade and macroeconomic policy-making, to help remove barriers to the integration of developing countries into the international economy;
- increase quality and, if possible, the volume of development

assistance. This requires focusing aid on human and social development, mobilizing private sector capital, continuing debt relief efforts for the poorest countries, and promoting democratic and structural reforms;

- improve donors' coordination and commitment from all the parties involved. The introduction of 'development contracts' (also involving commitments, from the receiving countries' side, on the broader mechanism of domestic governance, including education and military, and from the donors' side, on concessional aid, debt alleviation, market access) as well as the rationalization of the various UN economic organizations around a strengthened ECOSOC should be pressed forward;
- pay sufficient attention to the balance between macroeconomic stabilization, structural adjustment and long-term development. This means better cooperation between Bretton Woods institutions and, more ambitiously, between them and the UN economic bodies.

For the environment and its links with development, trade and finance

The environment is a relatively new issue-area (there was no recognition of the environment problem at the time of the setting up of the 'Bretton Woods' system). It is also, at least in important aspects, a truly 'horizontal' issue, as it involves developmental and trade aspects and, more in general, its consideration leads to demands for a re-orientation of industrial activity with attendant adjustment costs. A key problem therefore is ensuring that environmental considerations are given adequate weight in other policy areas; equally important is increasing the effectiveness of international environmental regimes, in terms of both commitments and enforcement mechanisms. Priorities in this issue-area are:

7

- make UNEP the true environmental pillar of the international economic order. It could become a 'World Environment Protection Organization'. This would involve the upgrading of the political representation of participants in the governance of the organization, and the setting up of an integrated secretariat for the elaboration and the follow-up of global environmental agreements. Although regional environmental agreements are sometimes more appropriate, there is a need for such an international body to set minimum norms;
- environment is also one of the 'new' policy areas with important links to the liberal trade regime. As well as taking forward current work in the WTO, the relationship between WTO and a reinforced UNEP must be developed;
- integrate more systematically the environmental dimension in all other policy areas. Because of the powerful links between environmental protection and other policies, environmental commitments will not be met if we do not mobilize all the necessary policy instruments. In particular, raising environmental standards in developing countries must be matched by better trade access and increased financial and technical assistance.

For macroeconomic policy and its links to trade, development and financial stability

Recent experience has re-emphasized that 'getting your own house in order' is a necessary but not sufficient condition for macroeconomic stability.

Free capital movements have meant global markets and increasing interdependence, but the rules of the game have weakened and efforts to make joint decisions generally failed. There is also a growing mismatch between global financial markets and national systems of supervision. Priorities in this issue area are:

- achieve stronger cooperation/coordination of macroeconomic policies among the countries of the reserve currencies. This requires agreement on objectives and commitment to use policy instruments to achieve them. This is a crucial condition for reducing long–term misalignment of key currencies, adjustment asymmetries and the negative interaction between macroeconomic instability and trade liberalization. The completion of EMU, which would create a new powerful reserve currency, is a crucially important factor for achieving this goal;
- set up better arrangements to help prevent crises in particular countries, and to deal with them better if they occur. A strengthened surveillance mechanism under the auspices of the IMF was endorsed by the 1995 G–7 Summit at Halifax and is a good first step;
- explore more systematic cooperation at international level between supervisors and regulators, and assess the adequacy of supervisory standards in all international markets. The proposed G–7 led review will be important in this respect.

MANAGING INTERDEPENDENCE: COMMON CHALLENGES FOR THE INTERNATIONAL ECONOMIC ORDER AND DIRECTIONS FOR INSTITUTIONAL ADAPTATION

The analysis of specific issue-areas, as well as highlighting important differences, in terms both of diversity of regimes and the relative strength of the institutional 'pillars', has confirmed some common challenges to:

- take account of more complex interdependencies while working with the grain of markets. Increasingly global markets impose new constraints on national policy-makers and demand international coordination related to previously domestic policies and/or to interactions between functional

9

areas. Ways forward include emphasizing transparency, mutual recognition based on core standards, and market-based instruments (e.g. eco-taxes);

- enhance the legitimacy of institutions, and of the system as a whole, while also increasing effectiveness/efficiency. The increase in interdependence and in the number of players poses obvious problems. Giving more players a say in decision-making must be accompanied by changes in decision-making arrangements that will increase effectiveness. This means associating the new economic powers and developing countries (greater rights and responsibilities) as closely as possible with the existing institutions and market economy principles but also developing more binding and more rule-based international regimes and finding ways of overcoming blockages (for example through decision-making by qualified majority or through regional constituencies);
- ensure implementation of, and compliance with, agreed rules, notably through strengthening of dispute settlement mechanisms where they are weak or non-existent. Restrictive general principles on cross-targeting (i.e. the use of policy instruments in one area to enforce undertakings in another area) and on action toward non-participants should also be as far as possible generalized. This should help to avoid recourse to unilateralism and contagion effects from one policy area to another.

The overall thrust of the analysis is that an increasingly interdependent global economy has to be reflected in the structure of policy-making. Greater coherence in national policymaking, and closer coordination between international institutions can help. But both have their limitations, not least that there is no means of resolving conflicts between policy objectives in different areas, or of developing a coherent overall framework (the G-7 representing, at best, a very partial answer suffering from obvious and increasing problems of legitimacy and effectiveness).

There is, however, much that can be done to strengthen the international economic order to provide overall coherence within the existing basic structure. Actions to improve legitimacy, effectiveness and implementation along the lines discussed above could also lay the basis for the development of some form of overarching structure, capable of reflecting the interests of the system as a whole and resolving conflicts across different policy areas and institutional mandates. Rather than advocating an all-embracing institutional solution the Report outlines a progressive approach to managing interdependence involving:

- strengthening the weaker pillars of the system (environment, UN economico-social bodies, macroeconomic policy) in their own right, and to reduce asymmetries in decision-making;
- making more serious efforts to deal with key existing interfaces, focusing initially on the priorities identified in the specific issue-areas. This should involve greater coordination between existing institutions (both at political and secretariat levels) This cooperation needs to be systematic, rather than *ad hoc*, and go beyond exchange of views, to common policy development on particular issues;
- giving a bigger role to existing institutions particularly apt to increasing coherence (CSD, IMF/WB Governing Committees, WTO, ECOSOC), including tasks of horizontal coordination and possible modifications of mandates;
- creating frameworks for coordination between multilateral institutions and national policies (e.g. through development contracts);
- increasing the involvement of regional groupings in policy coordination and integration in parallel with the extent of their functional competencies and their developing of efficient and legitimate structures;
- seeking to focus political interest on the question of whether

a move towards a structure to enhance coherence is desirable and feasible. This will need consideration of both the intensity of interactions and the need for greater legitimacy in the management of the system as a whole.

THE ROLE AND INTERESTS OF THE EUROPEAN UNION

The analysis and the conclusions of the Report had implications for the role and the interests of the European Union:

- the EU would be a major loser if, instead of a strengthening and extension of the multilateral system, the response to growing interdependence was bilateralism and protectionism. This conclusion rests on grounds not only of economic efficiency but also of broader risks associated with each regional grouping pursuing inward-looking strategies. Moreover the relative lack of EU political integration reduces the effectiveness of a bilateral approach *vis-à-vis* the US and/or Japan. At the same time, the EU also has an interest in ensuring that the development of international regimes is consistent with the European model, and not dominated by US or other approaches;

- the EU must combine continuing support for the principle and the practice of multilateralism with maintaining and developing a positive approach to regionalism; EU assessment of regional integration processes needs to take into account not only matters of trade or regional security but also aspects of global policy coherence;

- the EU is well-placed to take a leading role in developing solutions to the problems of interdependence at the global level because of its unique experience in dealing with integration and pooling of sovereignty at the regional level, which has posed many of the same problems, albeit with different intensity and with a strong commitment to political integration. Moreover, most of the key problems identified in the specific issue-areas relate to the first pillar of the Union (trade, development, the environment and [with EMU] macroeconomic policy) where Community competence and experience is established;

- but the EU will be able to take an effective role in establishing a more coherent economic order only if it can get its act together internally and thus be able to speak more often with a single voice. This was an issue for the 1996 Intergovernmental Conference (procedures for organizing 'mixed competence' between the Community and the Member States) but is also an issue in dealing with specific interactions (e.g. between IMF and WTO);
- the European Commission in particular has a special role to play in demonstrating the validity of European solutions to specific problems of interdependence and in preserving a long-term perspective on global developments in parallel with its long-term perspective on European integration.

Chapter 1

Framework of analysis

This part describes the current system and the major developments to which it needs to adapt; identifies objectives, and outlines the arguments for action at an international level; and sets out the main issues examined in the rest of the document.

1.1. INTERNATIONAL ECONOMIC ORDER IN A CHANGING WORLD

1.1.1. Characterization of the existing order

The international economic order is made up of a number of international regimes, that is, sets of principles, rules and decision–making procedures structuring the relations of states in the economic area. Such regimes have a common foundation in international law, which stresses the principles of sovereignty and equality of states as governing the international distribution of power.

The regimes comprising the international economic order are extremely diverse in membership, scope and institutional strength. Some regimes are virtually universal, others include only a limited number of participants; some are functionally limited to specific areas, others have the possibility of addressing a wide range of economic problems that are of interest to their members; some provide formal rules as well as enforcement mechanisms, others have less formal institutional arrangements that may provide opportunities for information and consultation but serve no enforcement role. This diversity is not an indication of weakness, provided each regime corresponds to the nature of the problem that it tries to solve. However, while some international regimes are recognized as being effective, others have drawn criticism for their lack of results. Also there is little or no coherence between the various regimes.

The post World War II economic order had growth and preservation of trade (especially trade in goods) as its primary objectives. Rules of the game generally sought to avoid tariff wars or competitive devaluations. Elements were built in to prevent global deflation. Little attention was given to development and virtually nothing to the environment.

1.1.2.   The historical context

The present shape of the international economic order is still largely the result of the major exercise in international constitution-making that took place at the end of World War II in connection with the establishment of the United Nations. In the economic area, narrowly defined, the product of that exercise was the 'Bretton Woods' system comprising a number of multilateral international agreements and institutions, most notably the General Agreement on Tariff and Trade, the International Monetary Fund and the World Bank (Figures 1 and 2). The ultimate objective of the system was to promote economic openness and growth as a necessary complement to collective security, bearing in mind the way in which economic fragmentation and politico-military hostility had fuelled each other in the period between the two world wars.

Historically, the Bretton Woods system can be seen as reflecting the interests of the states (in particular the US) which have played a dominant role in its design and management.

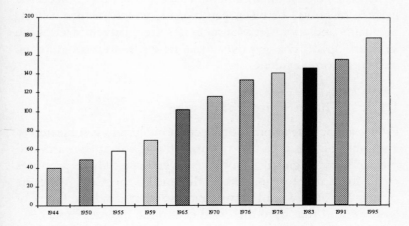

Figure 1. Number of IMF member countries
Source: IMF.

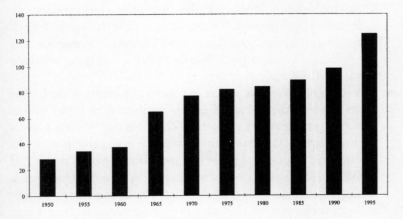

Figure 2. Number of GATT member countries
Source: GATT.

More generally, the international economic order reflects the balance of power between participants, which in turn reflects inequality and asymmetry of states. As the relative power of the key participants changes over time, new pressures for systemic reform become evident.

1.1.3. The pressures for change

Fifty years on, the international economic system is subjected to a number of pressures that require a fresh look at the rules and mechanisms of global economic governance. These pressures result from three major forces: the end of the Cold War; the emergence of powerful new economic actors; and the forces of globalization that have increased economic interdependence.

- *The end of the Cold War* means that international economic relations are no longer conducted against the backdrop of an overarching threat to the security of the market economies. This has greatly reduced the incentive to subordinate differences in national economic interests to political/ strategic preoccupations with the 'Western' consensus and has effectively decoupled North–South economic relations from Cold War alignments.
- *The rise of new economic powers and the relative decline of the United States* (and of the other 'Western' industrial powers) means that the power structure within the Bretton Woods system no longer reflects the current realities of economic power. As the unique position of power of the United States at the end of World War II has given way to the emergence of a multipolar world including regional actors, there is no longer a hegemonic power that can be relied upon to bear more than a proportionate share of the costs of enforcing cooperation.
- *The overall trend toward the globalization of markets* (most evident in the financial sphere) and the resulting increase in

interdependence (Figures 3, 4, 5, 6). Technological developments, and in particular improvements in international transportation and communication, interacting with the removal of barriers to trade and investment in the framework of the Bretton Woods system and changes in enterprise organization and strategy (flexible organization), have brought about a steady increase in structural interdependence, that is in the degree of 'openness' of economies toward each other. Structural interdependence in turn has resulted in increasing problems of policy interdependence, where the optimal course of action for one country depends on the course of action taken by other countries. It has also intensified the importance of interactions between policy areas at international level.

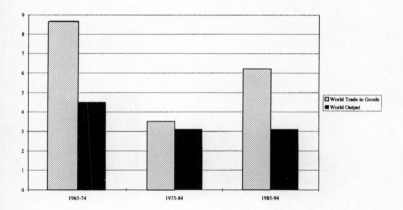

Figure 3. Growth of world trade output
Sources: IMF, *World Economic Outlook,* October 1995;
IMF, *International Financial Statistics Yearbook* 1994.

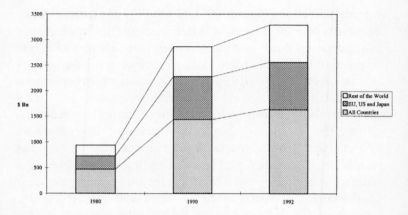

Figure 4. Stock of inward foreign direct investment
Source: European Commission, 'Trade and Investment', Directorate
General for External Relations, December 1994.

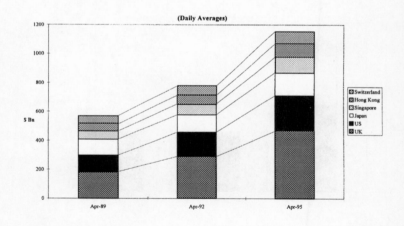

Figure 5. World foreign exchange market turnover
Source: BIS, *Annual Report 1994*.

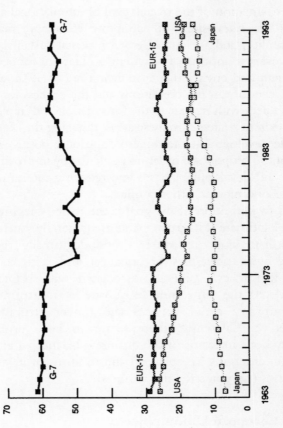

Figure 6. Share of world export of goods (at current prices and current exchange rates, excluding intra-EUR–15 exports)

Source: Commission database AMECO.

1.2. DEFINING THE GOALS AND ADDRESSING THE LEGITIMACY ISSUE

The notion of *sustainable development* – defined as 'development that meets the need of the present without compromising the ability of future generations to meet their own needs' – provides a good approximation of the overall goal of international action. It integrates the dimensions of economic efficiency, macroeconomic stability, and social and environmental sustainability. Its role, however, is not that of providing a blueprint for economic, development and environmental policies; rather, it should serve to focus attention on the conditions and the process for making rational choices with respect to the formulation and implementation of coherent strategies in these areas. Pursuing the objective of sustainable development should also contribute positively to the stability of the geopolitical order, in particular by improving living standards and development levels and reducing the number and scope of economic and other conflicts.

Linked to definition of the goal is the issue of legitimacy. A system is legitimate if its participants are generally satisfied with its decision-making procedures ('input legitimacy', generally associated with principles of equality) and with its results ('output legitimacy', generally associated with principles of efficiency). At the same time legitimacy is an attribute of an order, and any order reflects the power structure that established it. Currently, there seems to be a problem of legitimacy both in terms of the changing balance of economic power (i.e. emerging key players) and in terms of its enduring asymmetries (no voice for the weakest).

1.2.1. European Union objectives

From these broad objectives for any well-functioning international order, a set of more operational goals can be identified for the European Union, which include:

- preventing the resurgence of narrow-minded economic nationalism and the fragmentation of the world into competing blocs, which involves ensuring an adequate degree of stability at global level, and in particular macro-economic and financial stability which provides the necessary framework for growth and employment;
- maintaining and expanding an overall liberal regime for world-wide trade and investment as a crucial basis for our long term prosperity and employment;
- creating the conditions for a sustainable and successful development of developing countries;
- protection of the global commons.

1.3. DIRECTIONS FOR CHANGE IN THE INTERNATIONAL ECONOMIC ORDER

1.3.1. Approaches to dealing with increasing interdependence

While increasing economic interdependence is widely recognized to be the central force driving the development of international economic relations, there is no such general agreement on the shape that the international economic order is to take in response to the pressures that interdependence generates. There is also a tension between a world economy that is less and less segmented and a political order that remains highly fragmented.

From a conceptual point of view, two different broad approaches to dealing with increasing economic interdependence can be identified:

- *shallow integration*, involving increasing market access consistent with the maintenance of national sovereignty regarding non-border policies. In such a world there is, increasingly, free trade and freedom to engage in foreign direct investment. In the other areas countries retain their freedom of action, but do not pursue any discriminatory regulation of foreign products or producers, and compete on the basis of their natural endowments and regulatory regimes ('competition among rules');

- *deep integration*, in which governments are willing not only to further integrate their economies through liberalization but also to increasingly treat domestic regulatory policies and international interactions between policy areas as matters for international coordination and to provide for corresponding delegation of powers.

The real world exhibits a much greater diversity of levels of policy integration, in a number of dimensions: bilateral/regional/multilateral; exchange of information/consultation/coordination; competition among rules/mutual recognition-cum-minimum standards/harmonization. Overall, however, the foundations of the international economic order and its institutions remain closer to the first than to the second model, that is, 'shallow' integration predominates and the most binding international disciplines are those seeking to improve market access and reduce discrimination.

What can be said about the right balance between these different approaches? A first answer is that the degree of policy integration is and will continue to be conditioned by:

- the extent to which situations are perceived to require collective action; the perception of the need for collective action can evolve over time, not only in relation to the size of the associated gains but also to the attitudes of policy-makers and public opinions;
- the degree of similarity of the interests and the preferences of those involved. Because differences between countries tend to be greater than differences inside countries, there is a widely-held and in many cases well-founded presumption

that decentralized policy action will be more responsive to the needs of the populations.

This argument suggests a conclusion in terms of 'global subsidiarity': delegation of powers to international institutions should be limited to those functions that cannot be adequately performed by single states, or by cooperation between them. In terms of the two above approaches this means that competition amongst rules should be preferred unless there is a convincing case for coordination.

1.3.2. The case for enhanced international coordination

The economic argument for free trade provides a useful way of considering the extent to which the competition amongst rules implied by shallow integration should be preferred to enhanced international coordination. The general case for free markets relies essentially on the demonstration that competition results in the most efficient allocation of resources and thus in the maximization of global welfare. But there are also limits to the effectiveness of market mechanisms in achieving global welfare objectives, which also apply to shallow integration as a means of managing international economic relations.

The limits mean that there are strong arguments for international action to achieve common goals of sustainable development. Sustainable development is about both economic efficiency and justice in the relations between individuals and communities. Thus there are both efficiency- and values-based arguments for international action. Moreover, the pursuit of economic efficiency and justice requires a broader framework, and it is necessary to consider the extent to which this framework needs to be provided at the international, as opposed to national, level. The arguments for international action set out here need to be seen in the context of the perception of mismatch between national regulation and global markets, and the link with loss of effectiveness of national policy instruments.

International public goods

The international economy, like any other economy, requires a set of rules and mechanisms to ensure stability which, by their nature, are neither provided by the markets nor by governments acting in isolation. These rules and mechanisms can be described as *international public goods*.[1] Relevant examples include: systemic financial stability, the rule of law, including a widely accepted dispute settlement machinery, common technical standards and agreed systems to manage communication and transportation networks, and protection of the 'global commons'.

It is worth underlining that the definition of international public goods is subject to debate (e.g. some would argue that global macroeconomic stability is best achieved by 'each country keeping its own house in order').

One of the implications of increasing interdependence is the shifting of the boundaries between national and international public goods. Governments' traditional role in the provision of public goods will apply increasingly at international level or will otherwise become less relevant even at national level. In global markets it makes little sense to retain incompatible national standards, or to seek to ensure stability of financial markets exclusively at national level.

Economic efficiency

The efficiency case for international coordination relates essentially to the consequences of the fact that the activities of one state often affect the economy of another in ways that involve substantial uncompensated costs and benefits. In these cases competition may result in collective irrationality, that is, all being left worse off, and be detrimental to the efficiency of the economic system as a whole.

Direct spillovers present the simplest example: by-products of economic activity, such as pollution, in some cases affect only the country in which the activity originates, while in others have effects beyond national borders; the corresponding economic benefits, however, often accrue solely or primarily to the domestic economy; the fact that national governments may ignore the international consequences means that unilateral regulation of the activity will produce a result inferior to the joint optimum, such as more pollution than under a reciprocal agreement. But in the absence of a mechanism to ensure cooperation, countries will face an international 'prisoner's dilemma',[2] in which all are worse off by the pursuit of the interests of each.

Moreover, the structure of the world of nations lies far from what would be required to meet the conditions of perfect competition that assure the maximization of global welfare.

In real-world conditions there is the risk that national policy-makers might actually try to exploit the international spillovers of domestic policies as a 'strategic weapon' in economic competition. For example, industrial policies can be used to induce withdrawal from a sector where there is room for only a few competitors, or tax policies can be framed to divert capital flows. Mutual deployment of policies for international strategic purposes tends to be self-defeating, as countries end up in a situation which is worse than under cooperation for 'mutual disarmament': cooperation, however, is likely to require a coordinating instance (that is, some form of international governance), as each country retains an incentive to defect from its undertakings.

The existence of large asymmetries between countries also implies that the strongest countries will have a special incentive to engage unilateral action that, however collectively disadvantageous, might improve their own competitive position.

Justice

The working of the international economic order can be judged unsatisfactory not only on efficiency grounds but also with reference to a shared view of justice. Such dissatisfaction is often voiced in connection with increasing inequalities among and within nations and with violations of human rights.

Increasing inequalities in wealth among nations, associated with systemic barriers perpetuating asymmetries and preventing 'catching up', can be seen as detracting from the legitimacy and effectiveness of the international economic order. Power structures at the international level based on economic disparities may also tend to perpetuate those disparities. Similar arguments apply in the domestic situation of countries if the framework regulating international competition is seen as contributing to increased inequalities inside national societies and/or preventing the exercise of national regulatory preferences about what constitutes a 'just society'. Such dissatisfaction can be a factor inducing like-minded government to proceed further on the way of integration but it also raises risks of fragmentation.

Finally, arguments for international action can also originate from domestic political arrangements, resulting in the exercise of public policy in ways that conflict with widely-held moral values, most notably the respect of basic human rights. Such conflicts are liable to intensify as more countries, widely differing in level of development, political regime and cultural tradition, are drawn into the globalization process. Calls for collective action against violations of basic human rights are likely to become correspondingly louder, raising delicate issues of cross-targeting of policy instruments to achieve respect of agreed minimum standards and action against non-participants to such agreements.

However, persisting divergences of national preferences and situations as well as persisting incentives to defect in the absence of a supranational authority make it difficult to achieve such coordination, and raise delicate problems of regulating collective action toward outsiders and 'free-riders'.

1.3.3. Dealing with interdependence and interactions

These 'market failures' of the international system in terms of the adequate provision of public goods, the achievement of economic efficiency and the promotion of justice, provide arguments for coordination at the international level. These basic arguments are not new: what is new is the situation in which they have to be applied. In a more interdependent world:

- some national policy instruments have become ineffective as a result of the shift from national to global markets, and the domestic policies of others have become of increasing interest because of the impact they have on the conditions of international competition;
- the interactions between policy areas at the international level have become more intense, raising questions about the extent to which policy decisions in one area should take account of negative effects in other policy areas, and, more generally, how we can ensure that mutually consistent policies are pursued in inter-related areas.

So globalization generates a pressure for international coordination relating to policies formerly thought of as purely domestic in nature and to interactions between policies at international level. Like-minded governments become more inclined to pool their powers to make it possible to realize objectives that would otherwise elude them.

One aspect of this issue is the circumstances in which action might be taken in other policy areas, or against non-participants, to ensure the effectiveness of a particular policy. The first-best solution is obviously to achieve as wide as possible participation in international action. Taking action against non-participants, and even more, taking action in other policy areas (e.g. trade restrictions on environmental grounds) needs to be carefully justified because of the risks it carries of creating a vicious circle of new and worse distortions. These issues are considered further in part 3.

1.4. OUTLINE OF APPROACH

This chapter has set out a background and framework for the analysis of developments in the international economy and the indication of desirable directions of change in the international economic order. It has focused on increasing interdependence between economies, and the challenges that it poses in terms of enhanced policy coordination. The next part develops these general analyses in concrete situations in order to highlight specific options, in terms of instruments and institutions. The approach chosen is to focus on a number of specific 'clusters' or issue-areas. These clusters have been identified on the basis of what appeared the most important interactions arising out of work on particular policy areas. Four main such clusters have been selected, namely:

- 'new' areas or traditionally 'domestic' areas and their links with trade;
- development, and its links with macroeconomic stabilization, trade, the environment and migration policies;
- the environment, and its links with development, trade and finance;
- finance and macroeconomics and their links with structural adjustment, trade and investment.

Different institutional choices exist in trying to get to grips with these interactions, and in ensuring the coherence of the system as a whole. This set of choices will be assessed in the third chapter in the light of the work on key issue-areas.

Notes

1 Public goods are conventionally defined by two characteristics: (i) non-rivalry, meaning that consumption or use of the good by one 'individual' does not reduce its availability to anyone else; and (ii) non-excludability, meaning that once the good is provided, it is available to all. These characteristics contrast with the normal case of private goods, in which one individual's consumption precludes use by others, and where providers can ensure that only those individuals who 'pay' for the good may obtain it. In the case of public goods, however, provision left to competition is bound to fail because of the lack of such incentives. Even if the general benefit can be demonstrated, individuals have the incentive to act as 'free riders': to contribute less than their shares for the good but to gain from its provision by others.

2 The prisoner's dilemma refers to a situation in which the rational choice for each agent, acting regardless of what he thinks anyone else will do, is non-cooperation. But each one following such a strategy will lead to an outcome that leaves all worse off than if they had cooperated. The classic example is that of the two prisoners who may cooperate and keep silent (both thereby receiving light sentences), turn state's evidence, confess and go free (with the other prisoner receiving the heaviest sentence), or both confess (both thereby receiving moderate sentences). The rational choice for each prisoner behaving individualistically is to confess, so that both end up serving a longer time in jail than if they could have agreed to keep silent.

Chapter 2

Analysis of 'clusters'

2.1. 'CLUSTER' 1: 'NEW' AREAS AND TRADITIONAL 'DOMESTIC' AREAS AND THEIR LINKS WITH TRADE

This section focuses on how to deal with previously ignored or domestically treated policy areas that have become the focus of wider international attention. It considers the problem mainly from the angle of the interactions between these areas and the trade policy regime, with particular attention to the use of trade policy instruments for enforcement in other areas, and the possible scope for the World Trade Organization (Table 1).

For some issues the global nature of both the problems and the solutions has appeared very clearly. For others, it is the globalization of many markets and the growing interdependence among nations (Table 2) that has made more costly the inconsistencies and lack of coherence of national regulations. Hence, the widely perceived need for new 'rules of the game'. Among these issues, environment, competition, social standards and investment have received most attention.

2.1.1. Key problems in 'new' and traditionally 'domestic' areas

Much of the international discussion on the need for new 'rules of the game' and for better coherence among various policy areas has taken place in the international trade framework. There are three broad reasons for this. First, there are often clear linkages between trade and the new issues, especially since differences in national regulations are increasingly perceived to be a source of competitive advantage. Second, the GATT forum has proved to be quite effective in reaching agreements on difficult trade and trade-related issues, by giving countries the possibility of reaching a balance of concessions and gains across a wide range of issues. Third, trade policy instruments are seen as providing a readily available and effective means of enforcing international agreements in the absence of effective enforcement mechanisms in the policy area concerned. Their use can appear increasingly attractive as the trend towards a relative loss of effectiveness of regulatory power at the national level intensifies.

Hence, the key problems are typically related to conflicts or diversions involving trade objectives and other policy objectives. Specifically:

- *environmental standards*. High environmental standards can be a source of competitive advantage. However, the adjustment costs linked to the introduction of new standards, and the time lag and the uncertainty before the emergence of the competitive advantage of high standards, create incentives (especially in the developing countries) to give more weight to short-term competitiveness considerations favouring lax environmental policies. Also, openness to trade can exacerbate the effects of inadequate environmental policies (for example, trade in tropical woods). Different environmental standards across countries raise questions of adequacy of defence against spillovers, as well as of 'unfair' competitive advantages;

Table 1. The architecture of the World Trade Organization: the movement toward deep integration

MULTILATERAL
AGREEMENT ON
TRADE IN GOODS

	Tariff reductions on industrial products (weighted average)						Tariff bindings for industrial products (1) (excl. fuel)					
	All industrial products excl. fuel			Industrial products excl. textile, clothing, fish products			% share of tariff lines bound			% Share of imports bound		
	(imports from)						(imports to)					
Countries	Developed	Developing	Least Dev.	Developed	Developing	Least Dev.	Developed	Developing	Transition	Developed	Developing	Transition
General Agreement on Tariffs and Trade 1994 (GATT 1994) pre-GATT 1994	6.3	6.8	6.8	5.4	4.9	1.7	78	22	73	94	14	74
post-GATT 1994	3.9	4.3	5.1	3.0	2.4	0.7	99	72	98	99	59	96

Agreement on Agriculture

All non-tariff measures (quantitative restrictions, variable import levies, minimum import prices) to be converted to non-tariff equivalents (calculated as difference between domestic and world prices in 1986–88 period); resulting tariffs to be reduced over time; all tariffs to be bound at their new levels.

(1) Tariff binding: maximum level to which a country commits itself not to increase a tariff line, except by negotiation and compensation

35

Table 1. *Cont.*

Agreement on the Application of Sanitary and Phytosanitary Measures	
Agreement on Textile and Clothing	Multi-Fibre Arrangement (MFA), allowing imposition of quantitative restrictions on imports of textiles and clothing, to be phased out in 10 years; imports covered by MFA to be integrated into GATT.
Agreement on Technical Barriers to Trade	
Agreement to Trade-Related Investment Measures	*Trade-related Investment Measures (TRIMs) – restrictions of firms' imports to a given ratio of their exports (export-import linkage), firms production being required to contain a minimum of local inputs (local content) or to be exported – to be phased out (in 2 years for developed countries; in 5 years for developing countries; in 10 years for least-developed countries). Agreement applying both to foreign-owned firms and domestic-owned firms.*
Agreement on the Implementation of Art. VI of the GATT 1994 (anti-dumping)	Countries possessing anti-dumping legislation required to have in place judicial review mechanism independent from anti-dumping authorities. Assessment of existence of dumping to take into account product-cycle and other lag effects in relation to cost and prices.
Agreement on the Implementation of Art VII of the GATT 1994 (customs valuation)	

Table 1. *Cont.*

Agreement on Pre-shipment Inspection	
Agreement on Rules of Origin	
Agreement on Import Licensing Procedures	
Agreement on Subsidies and Countervailing Measures	*Export subsidies (subsidies contingent on export performance) and local-content subsidies (subsidies incentivizing use of local input) to be phased out, with no increase possible in the transition period. Other subsidies liable to request for compensation by injured countries. Non-industry-specific subsidies, R&D subsidies and regional subsidies not actionable.*
Agreement on Safeguards	'Grey area measures' resulting in restrictions on imports – voluntary export restraints (VERs) and Orderly Market Agreements (OMAs) – prohibited. *Application of safeguard measures to include 'public hearings and other appropriate means in which importers, exporters and other parties could present evidence and their views'.*
GENERAL AGREEMENT ON TRADE IN SERVICES	Agreement applying to measures by a Member State affecting consumption of services originating in other Member States. Four modes of supplies distinguished (i) cross border supply (no movement of supplier or consumer); (ii) consumption abroad; *(iii) commercial presence (FDI); (iv) temporary entry of natural persons.* Most favoured nation (MFN) rule applying to all services except those listed by each Member State (exemptions to be renegotiated in future services trade rounds, the first of which to take place within 5 years; negotiations on financial services, basic telecommunications and maritime transport to start immediately).

Table 1. *Cont.*

	National treatment (treatment no less favourable than that accorded to like domestic services and service providers) and *market access rules* applying only to sectors listed in each Member State's schedule, with possibility of maintaining limitations for each sector/mode of supply. Member States to provide information on regulations and practices respecting services covered by Agreement. *Member States to establish disciplines to ensure that qualification requirements, technical standards and licensing procedures based on objective and transparent criteria. Member States to allow for establishment of procedures for (mutual) recognition of licenses, education and/or experience.* Member States to refrain from restrictions on international transfers and payment for current transactions related to listed commitments.
AGREEMENT ON TRADE-RELATED ASPECTS OF INTELLECTUAL PROPERTY RIGHTS	*Member States to establish minimum standards of protection of intellectual property rights in seven areas: patents, copyrights and related rights, trademarks, geographical indications, industrial designs, layout designs of integrated circuits, undisclosed information. Transition period: 1 year for developed countries, 5 years for developing countries, 11 years for less developed countries (patent applications for pharmaceutical and agricultural products to be allowed immediately by Member States previously not providing patents protection for such items). Intellectual property disputes to be resolved under WTO's unified dispute settlement procedures.*
UNDERSTANDING ON RULES AND PROCEDURES GOVERNING THE SETTLEMENT OF DISPUTES	Dispute-settlement mechanisms applying to all matters covered by WTO. Disputes to be referred to panel with possibility of appeal to appellate panel. *Appellate panel's decision automatically adopted in the absence of unanimous voting against it.* Concerned Member State to implement panel's decision or to provide adequate compensation.

(*) Provisions in italics referring to 'non-border' policies ('deep integration').
Source: Commission Services elaboration from various sources.

Table 2. Employees involved in inward and outgoing foreign acquisitions (% of country's manufacturing employment)

Country	Year	Outward [1]	Year	Inward [2]
Australia	–	–	1987	23.8
Austria	1982	34.1	1958	36.5
Denmark	–	–	1986	12.4
Finland	1988	36.7	1988	8.4
France	1992	30.1	1990	16.4
Germany	1992	24.0	1992	17.0
Japan	1991	8.1	1990	1.0
Greece	–	–	1977	21.3
Ireland	–	–	1983	42.8
Italy	1993	18.5	1993	16.0
Norway	1981	2.5	1989	6.4
New Zealand	–	–	1990	23.7
Netherlands	1987	60.5	1987	14.0
Portugal	–	–	1984	12.9
UK	1981	22.9	1990	14.9
USA	1991	20.8	1991	10.8
Sweden	1990	47.0	1990	11.5
Switzerland	1992	95.5	–	–
Turkey	–	–	1990	3.2

(1) Number of employees in foreign associated companies of domestic groups as a ratio of the country's total domestic manufacturing employment.

(2) Number of employees in associated companies of foreign groups as a ratio of the country's total domestic manufacturing employment.

Source: S. de Nardis, *The Internationalization of Italian Industry*, mimeo, 1995.

- *social standards*. Differences in social standards and, particularly, differences between internationally agreed standards on workers rights (ILO conventions) and domestic practices raise questions of 'unfair' competitive advantages and basic human rights. The existence of important international externalities is less evident, even if migration effects can possibly be linked to social standards;
- *industrial, competition policies*. Ideally, industrial policy should deal with market failures and structural adjustment issues,

and competition policy should deal with monopolization, collusion and other restrictive practices. In practice, interest group and other considerations influence these policies in other directions. In an international context the absence of specific industrial policies tends to induce a distorted use of competition policy (for example, transnational application of anti-trust rules) and trade policy (for example, anti-dumping actions);

- *macroeconomic policies*. Persistent macroeconomic disequilibria at national level, and lack of coordination of macroeconomic policies at international level, may lead to abrupt fluctuations of real exchange rates and hence to swings in competitive positions. As well as inhibiting trade and investment, this can promote protectionist tendencies, with restrictive trade policies at home and unilateral trade measures designed to reduce trade imbalances. Conversely, there is the danger that a restrictive trade policy might induce some countries to pursue a strategy of competitive devaluation, with adverse effects for its trading partners and for overall stability.

2.1.2. Main negative interactions between 'new' and traditionally 'domestic' areas and trade

Trade policy-makers have already been confronted with the problem of potential negative interactions between trade policy and other policies (for example in the cases of preferential treatment for developing countries and so-called 'dual use' goods). These interactions are now stronger than ever. Many of the new issues are already on the trade agenda and, while in some cases substantial progress has been achieved, in others (e.g. on trade and environment) only some preliminary steps have been undertaken. Open issues include:

- *how to allow for the use of trade instruments* in agreements covering other policy areas, whilst ensuring it is compatible with the liberal trading system. Although there are legitimate uses of trade measures in the pursuit of objectives in other policy areas (e.g. the UN-agreed trade embargo on Serbia and Montenegro), trade policy-makers are concerned that their instruments are too often geared to other objectives, which might undermine the effectiveness and credibility of these instruments;

• *the unilateral use of trade instruments* in those areas where 'rules of the game' and/or effective enforcement mechanisms are inadequate at the international level could undermine the multilateral rules established in the trade area. It might lead to retaliatory measures and ignite political tensions, in particular between developing and developed countries as the latter face accusations of protectionism;

• *trade negotiations* themselves may be adversely affected as they might become subject to other policy agendas. It is therefore important to balance the wish to address the new issues and the interlinkages more effectively in the WTO with the need to prevent further trade and investment liberalization from being bogged down by inappropriate linkages.

2.1.3. Instruments and mechanisms

It is important to ensure that each issue, especially those which still lack proper 'rules of the game', is effectively addressed in an efficient international context. This might require setting up a new international regime where appropriate (e.g. in the environment field) or improving efficiency of existing functional arrangements as much as possible. Where 'rules of the game' do not exist, it is necessary to negotiate multilateral and comprehensive agreements. This is also the best way to avoid misuse of trade instruments.

For example, there is now a clear and widely recognized need for establishing a multilateral framework for investment. This is indeed one of the major policy priorities of the EU.

Similarly, the globalization of many markets and the extent of restrictive business practices call for the creation of a framework on adequate standards of competition law and their enforcement. Reaching agreement in these areas would meet the concerns of trade policy makers (i.e. maintaining the liberalization momentum and ensuring effective market access) while responding to the need of defining 'rules of the game'.

However, if a multilateral arrangement is not a realistic possibility in the short/medium term, an agreement should be sought among a more limited number of countries (for example, in the case of foreign investment, the EU has agreed to launch negotiations in the OECD before the issue is taken up in the WTO at a later stage) with a view to complement it by a wider (and more legitimate) agreement in a multilateral context.

A second key issue is how far the WTO could play a central role in setting 'rules of the game' in the areas where there are strong interactions with trade liberalization. This has already occurred in the case of the protection of intellectual property rights (TRIPs agreement) because an agreement could not be reached in the World Intellectual Property Organization. However, the strength of the links with the trade framework differs markedly from case to case. The link is clear and it is already established to some extent in the case of foreign investment. There is also a good case (based on externalities from 'strategic' use of policies) for integrating emerging international rules on competition law in the WTO context. The case is much less well based as regards social standards. When there are well-functioning mechanisms for defining standards at the international level (e.g. CITES), the WTO should not intervene in the definition of the principles.

Nevertheless, in those areas where there are no 'rules of the game' at the multilateral level or where there is a problem of non–compliance or non-participation, use of trade instruments is often contemplated (e.g. use of trade sanctions to enforce the

Montreal Protocol on ozone depletion). In some of the areas where rules of the game are weak, such as environment, and where it will take a long time to improve them, there may be a case for using trade policy instruments. However, unregulated use of these instruments might undermine the credibility of the trading regime.

So it is important to establish some general principles that can help decide if an interaction could usefully be considered in the WTO context.

First, the trade element should be sufficiently important. This apparently simple principle is, however, very difficult to apply in many practical instances. Second, once the trade link is established, the effectiveness of trade sanctions allowed for in the WTO framework and the extent of their impact on the issue itself and on world trade in general should be evaluated. Third, the burden of enforcement should not fall entirely on trade instruments; rather, use of other policy instruments should be considered (e.g. official aid flows, but see fuller discussion in part 3). Positive incentives should also be used in as many instances as possible. Last, but not least, when there is a consensus as regards the use of trade instruments, it must be ensured that they are as transparent as possible.

2.1.4. Institutional implications

The establishment of the WTO provides the multilateral forum for more effective action in the field of liberalizing and facilitating trade. However, the value of the WTO as an increasingly effective trade-focused institution could be put at risk and eventually lost by overburdening it with the tasks of not only reconciling different interests and priorities, but also of regulating a wide variety of fields. There is indeed a danger that the efficiency and legitimacy of the WTO's trade-dispute settlement mechanism will be jeopardised if it is involved in too many different policy areas. In order to improve the existing trading system, there are a number of important measures that should be considered for rapid implementation.

First, considering that the WTO should monitor the use of trade instruments, all international agreements providing for the use of trade measures should normally be made compatible with the WTO rules.[1] In the case of environment this could take the form of an amendment to Art. XX (dealing with 'exceptions') of the GATT so as to explicitly recognize that trade measures taken for environmental purposes are GATT-consistent if they are specifically provided for by a multilateral environmental agreement that is an expression of genuine international consensus. Any linkage between trade and labour standards should be conditioned to consensus at ILO level on definition and monitoring of basic rights of people at work (freedom of association and collective bargaining, ban on forced and children's labour).

In this context, effective collaboration between the WTO and the organization that oversees the agreement, in particular in order to define the 'rules of engagement' of the enforcement mechanisms (trade and other policy instruments), takes on special importance.

More broadly, in those areas where functional institutions exist, the first step is to strongly encourage greater cooperation. The aim is not only to improve contacts, increase awareness of issues, promote joint analysis and understanding (shared work programmes would be helpful), but also to devise consistent and coherent policy prescriptions and (as already noted) enforcement decisions. Enhanced cooperation between the Bretton Woods institutions and the WTO, already called for by the Marrakech declaration launching the WTO, could be extended to relations between the WTO and UN bodies with relevant expertise in social, development and environmental subjects (e.g. the Commission on Sustainable Development, ILO, UNEP, UNCTAD). A more rational division of labour between the WTO and the various specialized UN agencies would be especially appropriate. This would also help rationalize the system of international institutions by limiting duplication.

In one possible scenario for the longer term, the WTO in cooperation with the Bretton Woods institutions or under the auspices of an overarching body, might evolve as the key institution providing a regulatory framework in all trade-related areas and where interlinkages at the international level are important and clearly identified. In this case, it is clear that the current resources (financial and human) of the institution are not adequate to carry out vastly expanded tasks.

2.1.5.   European Union interests

The European Union is one of the leading proponents of the need to preserve and strengthen multilateral rules. By its very nature (a multicultural association of states) the Union is well equipped for pursuing trade liberalization in a multilateral rule-based context, while is ill-suited for result-oriented trade policy backed by unilateral measures. The Union thus has a strong interest in reinforcing the WTO framework. Accordingly, it has a strong interest in dealing with the issues and problems related to interlinkages discussed above. Moreover, the EU has an invaluable experience in dealing with the consequences of trade liberalization on other policy areas. This is an issue that was a direct consequence of the creation of a single market. We can therefore credibly propose our solutions, although it remains an open question whether we can apply, at the World level, the logic of European integration.

The EU has a particularly strong interest in ensuring that the WTO becomes an efficient and legitimate institution. Therefore, while in the short term priority to implement all decisions taken at Marrakech and consolidate the gains achieved in the Uruguay Round, it should be also recognized that the WTO provides the best available forum for discussing and reaching agreements on broader issues that interact strongly with the trade agenda. In addition, as the largest trading power in the world, the EU has a strong interest in a stable macroeconomic environment that would prevent protectionist tendencies from building up and hence undermine the liberal trading order. Effective cooperation between the Bretton Woods institutions and the WTO must be a priority, though the weakness of the IMF role in global macroeconomic policy limits the likely effectiveness of such cooperation in the short term (except perhaps in respect of exchange rate policy).

Consequently, it is important that the WTO membership be expanded to be truly universal and that it has the necessary technical as well as analytical resources to carry out its objectives. Strengthening the coordination and collaboration with other international institutions is a precondition for its effective functioning.

2.2. 'CLUSTER' 2: DEVELOPMENT AND ITS LINKS WITH MACROECONOMIC STABILIZATION, TRADE, THE ENVIRONMENT AND MIGRATION POLICIES

The growing importance of the development issue, also for the legitimacy of the international economic order, is simply illustrated by trends in population and income at world level, showing a decreasing demographic weight of industrial countries and increasing income inequality between the richest and the poorest countries (Figures 7, 8).

The extreme diversity of the development issue makes it almost impossible to make any observation which does not need to be qualified, for it is self-evident that the development of countries as diverse as the Czech Republic, India and Malawi have followed and will follow fundamentally different courses.[2] The following analysis is therefore not intended to be of

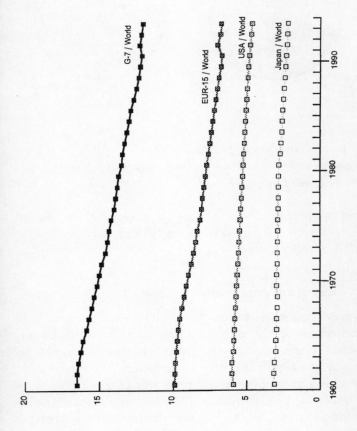

Figure 7. Shares of world population 1960–63 (percentage of total)
Source: Commission database AMECO.

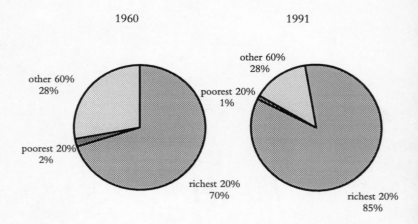

Figure 8. Distribution of world GDP[1]

[1] Distribution world population on the basis of per-capita national GDP.

Source: UNDP, *Human Development Report 1994*.

universal application. Nevertheless, it is possible to discern common themes within this diversity and that is what is attempted in this section.

2.2.1. Key problems in development[3]

Developing countries suffer principally from their lack of participation in the benefits of global economic growth and integration. The market system alone has no mechanisms for ensuring equitable distribution or equality of opportunity. Overcoming this problem is a central task of the international community. Certain transition and emerging economies are well advanced along this path – for many others the obstacles remain formidable. Some of these obstacles are the responsibility of the international community; others are that of the developing countries themselves. Among them it is possible to identify four important and inter-related problems. Two are largely exogenous problems, which primarily demand commitment at the international level and amongst the donor community as well as effort on the part of the developing countries themselves:

- *difficult international environment*: developing countries can find participation in the international economy difficult for three reasons: first, because the macroeconomic environment is unfavourable and unpredictable (e.g. in terms of developing countries' marginalization in capital markets and because of their particular vulnerability to macroeconomic shocks); second, because they continue to face systemic barriers to increased participation (e.g. continued marginalization in institutions, continued protection of certain markets, notably agriculture), and third, because they have not received the necessary support from the developed world (e.g. stagnant aid volume, inadequate technology transfer);

- *lack of resources*: public flows are stagnant partly because of budgetary constraints on donors and partly because of so-called 'aid fatigue'. There is also a genuine lack of certainty about the capacity of development assistance to achieve its objectives in the face of important systemic problems. The distribution of aid amongst beneficiary countries has, in the past, been distorted by the political considerations of the Cold War era and by donors' pursuit of commercial interests rather than developmental interests. These distortions prevent the most effective use of scarce aid resources.

Private flows are increasing (and now significantly outweigh public flows) but are narrowly focused on a few countries that could be considered as successfully emerging economies. The poorest countries and several transition economies have not, on the whole, benefited from this phenomenon (the extent to which the opening up of transition economies has diverted investment from poorer countries is debatable, but could be significant). Though the failure of many countries to attract private investment is often closely linked to domestic problems of governance, there is also a need for international action to ensure that those countries pursuing sound policies reap the benefits.

Two are more endogenous problems requiring essentially a continued commitment on the part of developing countries – with the support of donors – to good government:

- *unfavourable domestic environment*: transition economies have suffered not so much from under-development but from ideologically driven mis-development; in some countries political instability or war have prevented development in particular through the diversion of resources into the excessive expansion of the armed forces, in others, dictatorship or simple bad government have isolated countries from the global economy. In all of these cases, the effect has been the waste of national human and economic resources as well as the discouragement of the capital flows necessary for development;
- *under-utilization of human potential*: in most developing countries there are problems (to varying degrees) of non-participation in democratic structures; of discrimination against (or even repression of) women and minorities; of lack of education and of basic health care; of unemployment, and of the poverty which results from these and many other factors. These ills both undermine human rights and dignity and also prevent the fulfilment of human potential, including economic potential.

2.2.2. Key negative interactions between development and other areas

Economic growth is not the sole objective of governments nor of the international system. Nevertheless, the economic costs which often result from the pursuit of other legitimate objectives both at the national and global level (e.g. security, higher environmental standards) tend to be proportionally higher the poorer a country is. Developing countries are therefore particularly vulnerable to the negative interactions between economic development and the pursuit of other policy objectives. Specifically:

- *at the macroeconomic level*, the effects of interest rate and exchange rate fluctuations on the debt and balance of payments problems of developing countries are acute. Also, whilst no-one doubts the necessity of structural adjustment at the national level, it can have harsh medium-term consequences for human development, especially if excessive emphasis is given to the achievement of macroeconomic targets in respect of social and environmental costs;
- *the liberalization of trade* has eroded developing countries' preferential access to developed markets, whilst leaving certain important markets closed; this is particularly acute in the agricultural sector, where developed countries' agricultural policies continue almost systematically to undermine developing countries' domestic production. At the same time, the virtually free trade in arms fuels the instability that is a primary cause of under-development in many countries, and diverts human and financial resources away from productive investment. For some developing countries, revenue from the trade in drugs is an important part of GNP. The fight against drugs – and particularly the differing approaches of supplier and user countries to the problem – has significant development implications which demand greater international consideration;

51

- *dealing with past environmental problems* and preventing new ones are particularly costly for developing countries. In addition, some developing countries fear that higher global environmental standards may trap them in a state of under-development;
- *population growth, poverty and instability are powerful incentives for migration.* But in turn, the trend towards more restrictive immigration policies in developed countries has important economic consequences, as it militates against an efficient distribution of human resources, reduces the flow of capital to developing countries (from expatriate workers) and inhibits the development of cultural and commercial ties which can enhance trade and investment between countries.

These are not discrete problems – they can reinforce each other. Developing countries, and particularly the poorest, can find themselves trapped in a cycle of deprivation where, to take a very simple example, the lack of an educated workforce discourages inward investment which itself could be a source of government revenue which would fund education. To break such cycles requires decisive action, in particular by governments.

2.2.3.   Instruments and mechanisms

The powerful negative interactions identified above imply that the most effective action that could be taken would be to establish international mechanisms which, on the one hand, promote coherence between development and other policies and, on the other, deal with the negative effects of the pursuit of other policies where these are unavoidable (for a further discussion of institutional responses to interlinkages see 2.2.4 and parts 3 and 4).

As far as the specific problems of developing countries are concerned, there is already a range of policy instruments available, since development policy has long been recognized as a key aspect of the international order. But these instruments have not been fully effective. Two central problems have been the failure of conditionality to put pressure on for good governance and the lack of coherence with other policy areas. Changes are needed to remedy these shortcomings. In relation to the key problems identified above (2.2.1), the most important changes can be summarized as follows:

- *difficult international environment*: greater global macroeconomic stability would reduce many of the uncertainties which beset developing countries; more open markets for developing countries' goods (especially in agricultural products), and a greater attention to their concerns in international trade negotiations will promote their growth; support for regional economic integration can help especially the poorest to participate more fully in the global economy; concerted international action against the drugs trade, money laundering and other organized crime can prevent the squandering of developing countries' resources;
- *lack of resources*: encourage foreign direct investment through public leverage for private investment, including technical assistance for developing country governments, and through multilateral agreement on regulatory issues; reduce risks of sudden reverse capital flows through adequate international monitoring and better policy advice; concentrate public flows more effectively, match assistance instruments to needs more efficiently; increase, or at least maintain, public flows and make them more predictable, in particular by donors honouring their commitment to the agreed UN targets for levels of ODA, and through an adequate replenishment of IDA; reduce debt and stabilize external financial commitments; find efficient and just ways of stabilizing receipts from exports;
- *unfavourable domestic environment*: use political and assistance

leverage to promote and sustain democratic reforms; provide technical and financial assistance for programmes of economic reform which are tailored to the specific requirements of individual economies and which are supported by complementary policies in human and social development; use multilateral fora to encourage liberal and prudent domestic regimes for trade and investment;

- *under-utilization of human resources*: re-orient assistance policy around the objectives of poverty eradication, and of human and social development (including human rights); encourage domestic investment in human resources; focus the most concessional assistance on the poorest countries and the poorest sections of the population in other developing countries.

None of these approaches is new. However, two observations can be made about their use: first, their effectiveness is dependent upon developing countries themselves pursuing complementary domestic policies in partnership with the international community; second, they need to be used in a more coordinated way. Enhanced and realistic conditionality is one mechanism for encouraging the former; there is a variety of mechanisms (e.g. World Bank consultative groups, G–24 coordination) to achieve the latter.

One way of overcoming widely divergent approaches to conditionality and the lack of effectiveness of existing coordination mechanisms might be to establish 'development contracts' between the whole donor community and individual or groups of developing countries (both governments and representatives of the civil society), in which a partnership is established to use all international and domestic instruments in a coordinated way, in the pursuit of agreed policy goals. Commitments by receiving countries would not only refer to policies in the fiscal and the monetary areas, but also cover other factors such as: limitation of military spending; adequate health and educational systems; accountable judicial and governmental systems. Commitments from donors would refer to the whole range of policy instruments affecting the receiving countries, such as concessional aid, debt alleviation, market access, and could also take into account the overall macroeconomic environment and its effects on development objectives.

2.2.4. Institutional implications

The quest for increased legitimacy and efficiency is a key objective of the reform of the international order. For developing countries, the problem of the lack of legitimacy and efficiency in the international system is particularly acute. The legitimacy of the present order, so far as developing countries are concerned, is limited because their role in shaping it has been minimal and their concerns have been largely ignored, either for historical reasons, such as colonialism or the Cold War, or because of their lack of economic and political weight. From the point of view of efficiency it could fairly be claimed that the persistence, scale and profundity of poverty in an increasingly prosperous world is the most striking failure of the international system. Institutional reform must therefore take special account of these problems.

The legitimacy of the international order must be increased by ensuring that global policies result from a broad consensus of all – not just the economically powerful – democratic countries. The extension of WTO membership should be a priority. Equally, developing countries' representation, especially in the Bretton Woods institutions where their voice is very weak, should be re-examined. The global consequences of the work of institutions such as the OECD and the G-7 should be critically examined.

The effectiveness of development cooperation policies can be improved in a number of concrete operational ways (see above). Increasing and targeting assistance resources is vital, as is coordination between not only multilateral, but also national, donors. Here, the World Bank consultative group and G-24 mechanisms should be evaluated and, if necessary, improved (or scrapped); one might consider strengthening the coordinating capacity of one 'key-player' who might be different from one region to another. Such strengthening of regional coordinating capacity could also facilitate the conclusion of development contracts covering countries in a region.

The IFIs and the EU have a special role to play, as their continued commitment to development is symbolically as well as practically important. A clearer delineation of the IFIs' tasks with regard to transition, emerging and poorest countries is necessary, as is closer operational coordination between them and the UN development organs. For these, a reformed ECOSOC could provide a stronger political mandate and a much clearer policy context within which focusing and rationalization of the plethora of UN institutions could take place. It could then act as the UN's development voice in relations with other institutions.

The most important institutional question, however, is how to deal with the interactions identified above. Whatever institutional solution is proposed for this problem, it will only succeed to the extent to which it is founded on a genuine consensus about the nature of the world order and to which it achieves a more just balance between the interests of the people of the developing and developed world. This will not be easy.

2.2.5. European Union interests

The European Union has a particular responsibility for many developing countries, because of its Member States' historical links, because of the European vocation of the transition economies of central Europe, and because it is, for a majority of them, their most important economic partner. It discharges this responsibility by being by far the biggest source of official development assistance and by having some of the most generous preferential trade arrangements (e.g. through the Lomé Convention).

It is in EU interests to pursue active development policies, particularly with our near neighbours. Development assistance is also a means of ensuring market access for EU goods, and developing alliances with developing countries in favour of multilateralism. So it is both the EU's responsibility, and its vital interest, to press for more effective approaches to the problems of developing countries.

Its capacity to take on a full role is hampered by a lack of coordination within the Union (although this is very gradually improving). Strengthening the Union's own voice on development issues, especially in international fora, is thus in the interests both of the Union and of its developing country partners. It is also in the Union's interests to maintain pressure for the agreed UN ODA targets (of 0.7% of GNP for all ODA and 0.15% for poorest countries) to be met in order to achieve a more equitable distribution of the burden both within the Union and *vis-à-vis* other donors such as the US.

2.3. 'CLUSTER' 3: THE ENVIRONMENT AND ITS LINKS WITH DEVELOPMENT, TRADE AND FINANCE

The environment issue-area is relatively new, as public awareness has followed the development of the problems, so that the rules of the game are in the making. It was not recognized as an issue at the time of the establishment of the Bretton Woods system. The UN conference on the Human Environment, held in Stockholm in 1972, constituted the first attempt to launch a comprehensive process of international cooperation in this field and led to the establishment of the UN Environment Programme (UNEP) as an, albeit institutionally weak, environmental pillar of the international economic system. International environmental issues continued to have a low priority and were not properly recognized by the international community until the 1987 report, 'Our Common Future', of the Commission on Environment and Development chaired by Mrs Gro Harlem Brundtland.

The 1992 UN Conference on Environment and Development (UNCED) in Rio de Janeiro marked a turning point in efforts to protect the world's environment because of its far reaching results, namely the adoption of an action program to cover the full range of environment and development issues (Agenda 21), the establishment of the Commission on Sustainable Development (CSD) to monitor its implementation, the Rio Declaration on Environment and Development, the Statement of Forest Principles, the Climate Change and the Biodiversity Conventions.

However, the process initiated at Rio has lost some political momentum, partly due to the effect of the economic recession and the detraction of attention to other issues such as the problems of transition in the countries of the former Soviet Union. It is also important to bear in mind that the initial expectations were unrealistically high, ignoring that the transition towards sustainable development is a long-term process.

2.3.1. Key problems in environment policy

International cooperation in the environmental area is rather fragmented, both in terms of the participants involved and the subject matters covered. This is not as such inappropriate because regional agreements are, in many instances, the most effective way of dealing with environmental questions. Similarly, the sectoral approach that has prevailed in the development of international environmental law offers some practical advantages in view of the difficulties that the negotiation of more comprehensive agreements with a broader scope would involve. However, this fragmentation raises problems of policy coherence, also with respect to the treatment of non-parties.

Universal agreements are required to protect the global commons. However, the provisions in broad conventions with nearly universal membership tend to be highly general, reflecting a lowest common denominator only. Under these circumstances, implementation of environmental conventions is difficult to monitor and dispute settlement procedures are weak and seldom applied. The main reasons for the relative lack of effectiveness of most international environmental conventions are the consensus requirement, the difficulty of translating the principle of common but differentiated responsibility into a differentiated set of commitments and the lack of negotiating leverage within the environmental area. It is often difficult to satisfy legitimate requests for compensation by developing countries for the costs of higher environmental standards that could be in the form of financial and technical assistance, transfer of technology or trade concessions.

The institutional structure of the environmental pillar is weak compared to that of the other main pillars of the international economic order. In particular, UNEP is a programme, rather than an institution, with only limited competencies, a weak infrastructure and modest financial resources. Its effectiveness depends on voluntary contributions and political support of governments as well as cooperation with other bodies such as UNDP, the Global Environment Fund (GEF), the CSD and the separate secretariats of the various environmental conventions.

2.3.2. Key interactions between environment and other policies

It is increasingly recognized that adherence to the principle of sustainable development requires integration of environmental considerations into other policy areas. However, in practice this is difficult to achieve because of the functional compartmentalization of responsibilities. There are wide gaps between environmental protection and other policy areas, to the extent that the basic strategies for industry, trade and development are often evolving in complete isolation from environmental policy.

There is a strong interaction between industrial objectives and environment protection because sustainability demands an increasingly costly re-orientation of industrial activity that entails significant adjustment to economic structures and people's lifestyles.

The positive − as well as negative − interactions between environment and development have been recognized both conceptually and institutionally. There is, in particular, a developmental aspect to international action to protect the environment, in the sense that international targets based on present pollution levels would tend to require a much lower level of pollution per capita in developing countries. This would implicitly demand much higher standards of environmental protection in the countries that are least able to meet such standards.

More recently, the interlinkage of trade and environment has emerged as an important issue. The WTO, OECD, UNCTAD and UNEP have all done considerable work on examining the interlinkages between trade and environment. Free trade leads to the allocation of resources according to the principle of comparative advantage, whilst low environmental requirements tend to enhance industrial competitiveness in the short term. This situation leads to pressure for the use of trade instruments to compensate for differences in environmental requirements. It also provides arguments for intergovernmental action to establish international minimum environmental requirements for non-discriminatory trade.

2.3.3. Instruments and mechanisms

Environmental commitments and obligations in multilateral conventions need to be rendered more precise, and dispute settlement and enforcement mechanisms more effective. This may require a review of negotiation processes to overcome blockages due to a rigid interpretation of the unanimity principle. Also, the interconnection between enforcement and dispute settlement mechanisms in different areas (e.g. between environmental agreements and the WTO) needs to be examined.

Certain economic instruments for internalizing international externalities (such as environmental taxes, tradable permits or eco-management schemes) have been identified as appropriate mechanisms to deal with specific environmental problems efficiently and in a manner consistent with market principles. They may also generate resources to help implement the principle of common but differentiated responsibility. However, such instruments, so far, hardly exist because of a lack of political will and an inadequate institutional framework.

Chapter 2 of Agenda 21 stresses that environment and trade policies should be mutually supportive. Intergovernmental action to establish international minimum environmental requirements is, in principle, preferable to the use of trade instruments to compensate for differences on environmental standards, but in practice both strategies need examination to improve their effectiveness or prevent their abuse. A permanent WTO Committee on Trade and Environment has been established as the main forum for the resolution of potential conflicts, but its mandate is restricted to making recommendations for limited changes of the existing trade rules. It does not extend to the integration into the multilateral trading system of basic environmental instruments (on these issues see also 2.1.1, 2.1.3 and 2.1.4 above) or mechanisms to internalize environmental costs.

Despite acceptance of the principle of sustainable development, the interlinkages between development and environmental protection are not being addressed according to an integrated approach to sustainability. However, development policy takes account of the environment in several respects. Direct support for environmentally damaging projects is avoided as far as possible. However, multilateral support for macroeconomic stabilization and structural adjustment does not take proper account of the objective of environmental sustainability. A proportion of development finance is allocated to projects that are designated as environmentally beneficial. However, instruments to provide incentives for private financial flows in support of sustainable development are insufficient. Instead, the implementation of the principle of common but differentiated responsibility would imply that the industrialized countries should make available new and additional resources to cover the incremental costs of actions by developing countries aimed at solving global environmental problems.

Mechanisms to promote a better integration of the environmental dimension into other policy areas – such as fundamental environmental principles and effective monitoring mechanisms – are largely lacking. There is also a need to accelerate work on environmental indicators. The whole area of providing adequate funding mechanisms and financial incentives for sustainable development strategies needs to be reviewed.

Bilateral and regional agreements are often the most effective instruments for dealing with transnational environmental problems. However, in certain regions external support is needed to stimulate negotiation processes and overcome political blockages. Moreover, in order to deal more adequately with the problems of fragmentation (exclusion, free riders, compliance, coherence, etc.), such agreements need to be put in better interconnection with multilateral frameworks.

2.3.4. Institutional implications

The environmental area lacks an institution that would effectively stimulate and monitor international cooperation and norm setting. UNEP, in particular, would need to be strengthened institutionally and in terms of its resources to become a true environmental pillar of the international economic order. A minimum objective should be to establish a more common approach to analysis. However, a general environmental pillar on a par with other key institutions may require the establishment of a World Environment Organization.

The efficiency of the CSD, as the body in charge of monitoring and stimulating the implementation of Agenda 21, will also need to be improved. A better preparation of the annual sessions, a more focused debate and a more active involvement of development and finance ministers in addition to environment ministers would contribute to giving the CSD a higher standing.

The need to ensure the integration of the environmental dimension into other policy areas and to deal with interlinkages coherently may require some institutional changes within bodies such as the WTO, the World Bank and the IMF, as well as the improvement of cooperation mechanisms. In this context, international financial institutions, in particular the World Bank, should play a more active role in the field of the environment by fully integrating sustainability requirements into the project management cycle and by making resources available for environmental protection projects. Whether this would in, the longer term, be sufficient to ensure policy coherence or whether the promotion of sustainable development requires some kind of an overarching body is still an open question.

2.3.5. European Union interests

The Treaty on European Union includes, among the objectives of Community environment policy, the promotion of measures at international level to deal with regional or worldwide environment problems. In order to perform this task, the European Union must attach particular priority to the reinforcement of dialogue and cooperation with developing countries. The Rio Conference showed that a new partnership between industrialized and developing countries is needed to establish and implement effective strategies, to respond to global environmental problems and to achieve sustainable development. The European Union, by virtue of its moral, economic and political authority, can and should become the main interlocutor for developing countries, filling the gap left by other industrialized countries which lack the political will or the credibility needed to provide the necessary leadership in the field of the environment. This requires that the European Union has an adequate status within international organizations and speaks with one voice.

The EU has a particular interest in effective environmental standards: its experience on environmental issues will leave the EU in a strong position if global standards are agreed, whereas failure to make progress internationally may jeopardize the EU's regional efforts.

2.4. 'CLUSTER' 4: FINANCE AND MACROECONOMICS AND THEIR LINKS WITH STRUCTURAL ADJUSTMENT, TRADE AND INVESTMENT

The world environment in which economic and monetary policies operate has changed substantially, especially since the early 1970s. Apart from the collapse of the Bretton Woods fixed exchange rate system, the main changes have been the progressive move from an hegemonic towards a multipolar world and the emergence of powerful new economic players, the increased economic interdependence through globalization of financial markets (with restrictions on payments falling worldwide [Figure 9]), and the increased intensity of interactions between policy areas.

The Bretton Woods system worked in an asymmetric way, with the US playing the role of the key currency and of the economic motor. Now, the system needs to place more emphasis on global macroeconomic stability, which will require a new anchor. A composite (dollar, DM/Euro, yen) anchor could be a possibility. The three participants would have to agree to much closer coordination of their policies to carry out the anchor tasks. Requirements for greater discipline for the G-3/G-7 could facilitate a reinforced surveillance of emerging economies.

The discipline imposed by free capital movements and the globalization of financial markets create an incentive for better macroeconomic management. They also improve the allocation of savings. However, capital flows are not always driven by economic fundamentals and they can lead to overshooting and to greater asset price instability even if governments follow sound macroeconomic policies. The causes of this instability need to be addressed, focusing not only on the financial risks but also on the broader economic risks.

Macroeconomic stability at the international level can be considered as an international public good, being neither provided by the markets, nor by governments acting in isolation. Financial markets are global, but policy-making is essentially national. Traditional instruments of national macroeconomic policy-making have lost much of their effectiveness. The main variables, such as interest rates, are increasingly global.

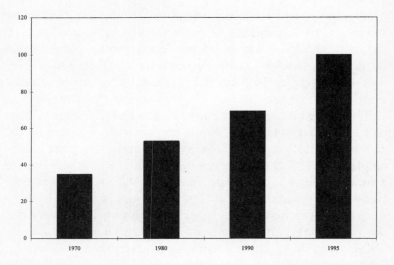

Figure 9. Number of countries with convertible currencies[1]

[1] IMF Member Countries accepting Art. VIII obligations on currency convertibility on current account transactions.
Source: IMF, *International Financial Statistics*, various issues.

2.4.1. Key problems in finance and macroeconomics

In the world environment of exchange rate flexibility, absence of credible commitments to stabilization and globalized financial markets, two key inter-related problems have emerged:

- *macroeconomic stability of the international system and lack of anchor.* Economies of scale in the use of money mean that only a few currencies are effectively used at a world level in any period in time. World liquidity is largely market created, with macroeconomic stability for the international monetary system largely dependent on the policies of the G-3 countries. The economic and monetary policies implemented by these countries have a central impact on international stability. Upward and downward shifts in the supply of key currencies (up to now, mainly the dollar) have been liable to trigger cycles of worldwide monetary contraction and expansion. In the present system there is no effective 'nominal anchor' which regulates the growth rates of convertible currencies;

- *sound national economic policies are not sufficient to lead to global stability*: the key currency countries use their policy instruments (monetary and fiscal) to influence domestic macroeconomic conditions, taking little, if any, account of the impact on international stability. They tend to consider that international stability should result naturally from sound domestic policies. This approach takes insufficient account of policy spillovers in the area of macroeconomic stabilization working through increasingly integrated goods and capital markets. For example, a tight monetary policy in one of the major players corresponding to its domestic situation may lead to high interest rates and/or depreciation in other countries leading to policy dilemmas; or national macro-economic programmes financed through short-term debt and volatile capital inflows may lead to a financial crisis involving not only the recipient country but others, world-wide.

As capital flows are not always driven by fundamentals, their discipline may not be appropriate or not applied smoothly. Asset price instability is likely to arise even if governments follow sound macroeconomic policies. The instability may be expressed through short-term volatility or, probably more important, large-scale and long-lasting overshooting in the price of financial assets.

2.4.2. Key negative interactions between finance and macroeconomics and other policy areas

The increased intensity of interactions between globalized financial markets, national macroeconomic policies and other areas can be seen through a number of problematic links or constraints. Specifically:

- *constraints of high capital mobility on national macroeconomic policies*: in an environment of integrated financial markets, even the floating exchange regime seems to have lost its originally assumed power to insulate one economy from the effects of the monetary policies pursued elsewhere (Table 3). At a global level, any commitment on macroeconomic stability requires the acceptance of some constraints on national macroeconomic policies, both fiscal and monetary;

Table 3. Interest rate correlations

| | 10 year bond yields: correlation with the US | | | |
	1970–79	1980–84	1985–89	1990–94
Japan	0.38	0.18	0.67	0.96
Germany	−0.24	0.78	0.65	0.93
UK	0.63	0.60	0.54	0.96
Canada	0.94	0.93	0.98	0.97
	10 year bond yields: correlation with Germany			
	1970–79	1980–84	1985–89	1990–94
France	−0.14	0.79	0.47	0.97
Italy	−0.54	0.54	0.69	0.74
UK	0.12	0.77	0.69	0.94
Belgium	−0.12	0.83	0.74	0.96
Netherlands	0.52	0.90	0.88	0.99
Sweden	−0.61	0.54	0.61	0.88
Switzerland	0.86	0.88	0.74	0.91

Source: Commission Services.

- *link between structural adjustment and macroeconomic stabilization*: fundamental structural imbalances in a country may jeopardize apparent success in the macroeconomic stabilization field, leading to a sudden reverse in capital flows. The current system of surveillance cannot prevent such situations, which can also undermine international economic stability. The linkage also works the other way: macroeconomic stabilization policies may undermine structural adjustment or long-term development (e.g. by reducing resources for long-term investment). More broadly, if world monetary conditions are too easy, adjustment will be delayed and there will be an overall inflationary tendency. Conversely, if monetary conditions are too stringent, adjustment will be excessively harsh and costly. The system of international liquidity also discriminates against poor and non-creditworthy countries;
- *link between macroeconomic instability and development*: interest rate instability increases the difficulties of debt management. High interest rates linked to instability reduce the room for manoeuvre of developing countries to use the available resources. Developing countries are particularly vulnerable to macroeconomic shocks;
- *link between exchange rate and interest rates' instability and trade*: exchange rate variability has increased the risk associated with international trade activity, thus arguably reducing its volume. The exchange rate can be used by certain countries in conjunction with policies of financial protectionism as a tool to gain competitiveness, with a direct impact on trade and indirectly affecting the macroeconomic situation;
- *risk of systemic failure of the financial system*: the current supervisory and prudential rules do not seem to have adapted rapidly enough to the globalization of financial markets, including the development of new instruments and new types of financial intermediaries. This entails a risk for macroeconomic stability at the international level. To the extent that central banks, as lenders of last resort, act to

prevent an imminent default of financial institutions, price stability may be undermined due to excessive creation of liquidity. On the other hand, when the financial sector is in serious distress, a credit crunch could hamper the picking up of economic activity;

- *constraints on domestic tax policy*: financial integration and capital mobility tend to put downward pressure on capital tax levels because of the incentive to invest in low tax jurisdictions. This can tend to shift the burden of taxation from capital, leading to a distribution of taxation that is inefficient from the global point of view. This in turn can aggravate social tensions, and create resistance to liberalization.

2.4.3.   Instruments and mechanisms

The powerful negative interactions that can develop between macroeconomics and other policy areas call for strengthened international cooperation and coordination in a number of areas. Specifically:

- *reinforced surveillance*: surveillance could be reinforced by strengthening the analytical support provided by the IMF, by identifying early enough potential inconsistencies, and giving more persuasive advice on how to avoid or correct the problems. In order to make surveillance more effective, some kind of instrument giving IMF more leverage might be appropriate. However such an facility does not address the problem of large key players pursuing unsound policies, or failing to cooperate, and improved surveillance within the G-7 is also highly desirable, perhaps drawing lessons from Community experience. Increased transparency could also reinforce surveillance. Options to increase transparency include: (i) improved accounting and disclosure standards (including reserves, debt, etc., now agreed by G-7),

(ii) publication of Article IV reports and other forms of IMF surveillance, (iii) greater G-7 finance communication to markets;

- *macroeconomic policy coordination*: this would be a longer-term and more ambitious option. The key issue in any system of coordination is the credibility and the willingness of the authorities to use macroeconomic policy instruments in support of objectives agreed at the international level (which could involve more effective control of world liquidity). Coordination would have to rely on an agreed analytical framework. The authorities would need to agree on targets, either final (e.g. inflation rates) or instrumental (e.g. exchange rates). If the actual values are out of the target ranges, national authorities would at least have the obligation to question their economic policies, and perhaps modify them, depending on the degree to which the agreed regime requires automatic policy responses, or leaves a degree of discretion. Coordination could be based on a single instrumental target (exchange rate or monetary aggregates) or on an agreed list of economic indicators ('monitoring zones'). Whatever the instrumental target used, economic and monetary policies have to be consistent with the target;
- *improving financial markets supervision*: adequate structures of supervision and global channels of information exchange and cooperation between banking, securities, insurance and other financial supervisors should be developed, particularly where financial conglomerates are concerned. The EU may provide a model. A more formalized structure of cooperation could be envisaged to cover issues like legal restrictions on exchange of information, opening 'gateways' for the exchange of information between supervisors, and how to integrate, at the international level, regulatory systems which are based on different technical approaches and represent different constituencies.

Supervision standards should be reinforced in all the

71

international market places, in order to avoid 'race to the bottom' and overcome the serious risk that supervisory techniques lag some way behind market practice, notably as markets can and do move and change rapidly. The review requested at the Halifax G-7 Summit is a potentially important way of making progress here;

- *action against money laundering*: international cooperative efforts should be reinforced by formal legal instruments. Further research should be encouraged (already promoted by the IMF and BIS) on aggregate data on the extent of money laundering and the distribution of its proceeds, on the links between money laundering and under-development, and on the inter-relationship between money laundering and tax evasion. Some form of control on deposits in tax havens should be envisaged. Thus, progress requires a combination of better international regulation, and common international action, including coordination of national policies.

2.4.4. Institutional implications

This section is devoted mainly to ideas to enhance macro-economic policy coordination, given the weakness of this pillar in the current international system:

- *changes within the IMF:* the IMF Interim-Committee should play an increasing role in decisions related to surveillance and macroeconomic stability. The Committee could probably work more effectively if substantive discussions could link better with work at Executive Board level. The Executive Board should reinforce the multilateral aspect of the current bilateral-based surveillance of the IMF. Special obligations for the G-7 countries within the surveillance exercise could be envisaged. This would imply a need for stronger coordination between the G-7 and the IMF;
- *reinforcement of cooperation between institutions (IMF, World Bank*

and WTO): cooperation, particularly between the IMF and the World Bank, should contribute to ensure consistency between macroeconomic developments in the leading economies (mainly exchange rates and interest rates) and the adjustment process (mainly in developing countries). As a starting point, these institutions should produce common analytical work on overlapping issues. A more fundamental change would be for the institutions to jointly define some 'binding' orientations to be applied. There is also scope for rationalization through improved cooperation, both at working level and at the decision-making level.

Cooperation between IMF, World Bank and WTO would be particularly relevant in the context of a surveillance procedure within a target zone framework. The use of the exchange rate as a trade weapon in connection with financial protectionism should also be examined together by those institutions. Also, in the case of liberalization of financial services, cooperation would reduce the risk that liberalization could adversely affect macroeconomic stability;

- *strengthening the ties between the various bodies of supervisors*: though supervisors remain, broadly speaking, supporters of retaining informal links, some degree of formalization will be needed. It should ensure installation of effective international rules and procedures which preserve confidentiality and professional secrecy and enable effective cooperation;

- *institutional change to facilitate increased coordination*: the institutional changes set out here provide one approach to increased macroeconomic policy coordination. This should be seen in a long-term perspective, given that there is no current willingness amongst the G–3 to intensify cooperation on these issues. It is important for an institutional setup that it can operate efficiently and ensure legitimacy. This is a particularly delicate issue for macroeconomic stability, given that there is still a relatively small number of key players. In any institutional changes, this would need to be recognized, while ensuring that the G-3/7 do not impose a particular approach on all other participants. The functions to be performed, either by a single institution or by a range of them, are mainly: (i) to provide analytical support so as to underline participants' commitment to the system and to lock them in to the process of coordination; (ii) to move from *ad hoc* to consistent coordination, (iii) to manage process and instruments (i.e. secretariat and executive functions). A possible option, in term of institutional division of labour, could be the following:

- *Analytical support*: IMF. This would be an extension of a function already performed by the IMF for the G-7; it could involve regular assessment of equilibrium exchange rates;

- *Decision-making*: combination of IMF and extended G-7 finance. As well as distinguishing decisions on system design from decisions on its operation, there would also be a need to look carefully at how a G-7 operational function could be reconciled with an IMF validation function;

- *Secretariat/executive*: it is clear that under any scenario either the G-7 would need to be more institutionalized, or a new institution would need to have more institutional back-up than the current G-7, but whether this should be limited to secretariat functions, or extended to executive functions (administering target zones) is an open question, since this function could also fall naturally on the IMF (it was its central function under Bretton Woods system).

Any option should take into account the need to involve central banks, since any type of arrangement on macroeconomic policy coordination involves monetary policy. Since central banks are becoming more and more independent and are, in some cases, solely responsible for monetary policy, they have to be involved in the process.

2.4.5. European Union interests

The European Union has a vital interest in macroeconomic stability both within the Union and at the global level. Indeed, macroeconomic instability, usually reflected through exchange and interest rate instability, has a negative impact on the integration process. Instability at global level can result in instability within the EU. This can put into question the single market itself if it goes too far. In addition, the Union as the major trading partner in the world has an interest in an environment where the adjustment mechanism works efficiently.

Within the Union, a certain number of instruments have been developed to address the issues of macroeconomic and financial stability, and to preserve free and open markets together with increased integration. Concerning macroeconomic stability, the Union has a system of multilateral surveillance that aims to ensure the consistency between macroeconomic policies of Member States. This approach, which includes agreement on objectives, national programmes to meet these objectives and strict monitoring to identify, through collective discussion, when and why programmes go off course, is relevant at the international level, although it cannot be automatically transposed.

Regarding financial stability, the Commission is competent in the field of financial regulation, covering the sectors of banking, insurance and securities. Therefore, the Commission can have an important role providing expertise in harmonization of both prudential rules within, and across, these sectors.

Notes

1 A further problem is the case of existing international agreements that contain WTO-incompatible trade measures.
2 A useful, if crude, distinction between 'transition', 'emerging' and

'poorest' economies is used throughout the paper, with 'developing' being used (albeit unsatisfactorily) as an umbrella term.
3 This paper will not discuss humanitarian assistance.

Chapter 3

General issues and institutional choices

In this chapter we seek to draw out some general lessons from the subcluster work, and assess horizontal issues in the light of the results.

The cluster work illustrates the growing interdependence between countries, and interactions between policy areas, and demonstrates that current approaches are not well adapted to dealing with these interactions. But it should also be noted that:

- The situation, and thus the right approach, differs very much between one policy area and another. Different arrangements in different areas, combined with differences in membership of different regimes, inevitably means that a degree of mismatch at interfaces is inevitable, and makes dealing with interactions more difficult.
- The relative strength of the 'pillars', i.e. the institutions of the international economic order differs: in some areas a prerequisite of dealing more effectively with interactions may be to strengthen individual pillars (e.g. trade/macro-economic interactions require a stronger role for IMF in macroeconomic policy).

The cluster work confirms the importance of three sets of complex problems:

- How to take account of more complex interdependencies while working with the grain of global markets;
- How to enhance the legitimacy of institutions, and of the system as a whole while also increasing effectiveness/efficiency.
- How to ensure effective enforcement and avoid recourse to unilateralism and contagion effects from one policy area to another.
- In this chapter these three challenges are closely examined, and some recommendations for responding to them made (3.1); interactions from an institutional perspective, with a view to striking a balance between efficiency and coherence, are then considered (3.2).

3.1. THREE CHALLENGES FOR THE INTERNATIONAL ECONOMIC ORDER

Running through much of the discussion of these challenges, in one way or another, is the issue of national sovereignty: the global nature of markets is one factor pushing for far greater policy actions at global level. Efforts to deal better with interactions, at the international level, may take decision-making further beyond national control; one objective of effective international regimes is to remove the scope for (as well as the need for) unilateral action, and this is sensitive in some countries (e.g. the US). The pooling of sovereignty is an issue on which Europe clearly has some experience but it remains sensitive both for its members, and for other key players.

3.1.1. Coping with interdependence and global markets

Two general trends can be identified:

- *the importance of learning to live better with global markets*: the fact that some markets operate increasingly at a global level imposes new forms of discipline on policy-makers (particularly on macroeconomic policy) and requires new international cooperative solutions that work with the grain of markets (e.g. economic instruments in environment, improving information flow, private sector led regulatory/ standards work etc.). Markets are also highly interdependent, implying that regulators and policy makers need to recognize these inter-relations and impact of their policy instruments in other policy areas (e.g. impact of trade tensions on exchange rates);

- *the growing case for 'deep' integration*: more markets becoming global and more policy areas becoming international demand international coordination of what were previously domestic policies, and require that interactions between functional areas (and thus between functionally specific institutions) are given more weight. Thus:
  - environment, investment and competition policy are no longer seen as purely domestic policy issues, partly as a result of trade liberalization. This has the effect that coordination is needed in these areas to achieve objectives that can no longer be achieved by national policy instruments, and that differing national rules in these areas can distort trade patterns and frustrate objectives of trade liberalization;
  - there has been an intensification in the extent to which national macroeconomic policies are interdependent (measured, for example, in terms of the extent to which long term interest rates move together), with more serious adverse consequences if they are inconsistent. These consequences are felt in trade and development, as well as in economic policy;
  - development policy has been hampered by its isolation: achievement of the objectives of development policy depends as much on appropriate global macroeconomic

and trade policies as they do on traditional 'development policy' instruments;
- dealing with global environmental concerns means taking them into account in trade, development and financial policy formulation.

The case becomes even stronger if a range of other issues with an economic dimension – global crime, money laundering, migration – are also taken into account. One key argument for deeper integration is that it is the combination of greater interdependence, and the pursuit of more complex objectives, such as sustainable development, that requires a move beyond minimalist solutions, and a combination of agreed rules of the game, and even collective policy-making, at international level.

It is important that these two developments (markets and interdependence) are addressed together. In some respects they are complementary: markets are global, and there are no artificial barriers between different policy areas, so that the basic logic of 'deep' integration can itself be seen as 'market-driven'. But there is also a potential conflict between these two developments, since the power of markets limits the choice of the form of deep integration. The challenge is to devise solutions to problems of collective action posed by inter-dependence that are effective and which minimise distortions to markets.

Bearing in mind the general conclusion in terms of 'global subsidiarity' that underpins our analysis of interdependence, helpful criteria in dealing with the challenges include:

- *increasing transparency*: market failures can arise if markets have insufficient information on which to base decisions. This is particularly true of financial markets and their assessment of national macroeconomic policies. But it could also be a useful criterion in dealing with institutional conflicts arising from diverging mandates, given that a key step in resolving negative interactions is for participants to recognize their existence;

- *extending mutual recognition based on 'core' standards*, rather than insisting on the stark choice between competition among rules and harmonization. But such an approach requires a commonly accepted standard-setting procedure as well as effective monitoring and compliance mechanisms, all of which tend to imply a fair degree of mutual knowledge and trust. It also requires the establishment of mechanisms to safeguard the legitimate objectives and interests of countries with high standards (e.g. in the field of the environment);
- *more binding coordination of national policies and capacity for common decision-making* (e.g. macroeconomic policy, environment).

3.1.2. Improving legitimacy and effectiveness

Legitimacy is bound to be an increasingly sensitive issue at international level, as every move toward 'deep' integration means that previously domestic policies become the subject of international action. Sensitivities about national sovereignty need to be addressed in this respect, which means, *inter alia*, convincing political actors and public opinion of the importance of dealing effectively with growing interdependence. Effectiveness has always been recognized as one of the crucial problems of international regimes and the analysis by 'cluster' provides several illustrations of this (for example, concerning the weaknesses of the environment or the development 'pillar').

There is a substantial complementarity between legitimacy and effectiveness, as institutions that lack legitimacy are unlikely to be effective in the long run. Similarly, a regime that is not effective in achieving its objectives will lose support and thus lose legitimacy. At the level of decision-making procedures, however, the two are often seen as conflicting, as reaching decisions is made difficult or sometimes impossible by excessive interpretations of consensus or use of veto powers presented as requirements of legitimacy. Among the requirements of legitimacy is that all members or groups of members should have a say in decisions; the relative weight of the players should also in some way to be reflected if decisions are to be sustained by effective implementation. But this does not mean unanimity. Nonetheless, the need to include more players in the decision-making process and achieve broad consensus, inevitably makes effective decision-making more challenging.

A central conclusion is therefore that:

- Giving more players a say in decision-making must be accompanied by changes in decision-making arrangements that will increase effectiveness. There is a parallel here with the process of EU integration, where the next IGC will focus on more effective decision-making in a Union with more members.
- In addition, the need to give all a say in decision-making has to be balanced against the need to reflect the reality of the distribution of economic power and changes in it; otherwise decisions will not get implemented. (The support the developed countries have given the IMF and World Bank, compared with that given to the UN economic bodies, reflects in part the greater weight in decision-making they have in the former bodies. The principle of 'one country, one vote' remains too distant from power realities).

A number of changes can be envisaged to achieve both greater effectiveness and legitimacy in decision-making. Possible approaches include:

- *favouring open-ended regimes as opposed to closed clubs* to avoid risk of abuse of power by self-selecting 'elite' states. Universal membership is a requirement for bodies with global responsibilities, especially in areas in which the risks of 'free-riding' are substantial;

- *greater recourse to rule-based international regimes*. The underlying argument is that it is more efficient to negotiate a set of rules, which can be applied to individual situations, than undertake negotiations each time a specific problem comes up. (Thus the GATT, which is rules based, has proved able to remain effective with growing membership). This argument becomes more compelling with the increase in the number of players involved;

- *progressivity, that is, the linking of the structure of decision-making to the degree of involvement in the international economy*, and changes in it (and, perhaps, involving some conditionality in respect of democracy). There is a particular need to look again at the way this principle is applied to the voting arrangements of the Bretton Woods financial institutions. The upcoming review of the quotas on which votes are weighted is relevant here. The current debate on expanding the General Arrangement to Borrow illustrates the difficulty of persuading existing members of the 'club' to accept this principle;

- *the balance of representation of countries be improved*. This would be achieved efficiently through regional constituencies (for example, the Global Environment Facility, working with a membership of more than 100 states and a governing body of 32 members, each representing a constituency, or the IMF and World Bank Executive Boards). This would also provide an incentive for regional cooperation, provided the representative of a regional constituency speaks on behalf of all its members;

- *exploring ways to overcome blockages* (particularly in the negotiation of new rules) due to a strict application of the unanimity principle by resorting to more flexible interpretations of consensus, allowing decision-making by a qualified majority of participants;

- *strengthening policy initiation capacities* by the heads of the relevant organizations and/or representative core group bodies.

3.1.3. Ensuring implementation and compliance

A key advantage of effective international regimes (sound rules and effective enforcement) is that it reduces the risk of extra-territorial application of domestic policies or of unilateral enforcement of international obligations (notably through trade measures). A failure of enforcement in one policy area can undermine multilateral rules in another area (e.g. unilateral trade measures for environmental protection that flout WTO rules). Two particular issues need to be addressed to help reduce these risks:

- *cross-targeting*, that is, the use of instruments in one policy area to enforce undertakings in another area;
- the extent to which *enforcement action* can be taken *against countries which are not signatories to an agreement*, but whose action may risk undermining its effectiveness. For example, achieving the objectives of certain agreements in the environmental area may require action toward countries that are not party to the agreements, in order to avoid such countries strategically exploiting their non-participation.

The initial question is how to make each functional regime effective. In the first instance, this is a question of improving the efficiency of surveillance and dispute settlement mechanisms under the various legal regimes. However, this may not be adequate in the absence of effective enforcement mechanisms. Some policies lend themselves to enforcement action more readily than others. Thus, for example, trade policy instruments provide a means of responding to breaches in trade rules, whereas there are no obvious instruments available in the social field for enforcing internationally agreed labour standards.

The use of trade policy instruments (discussed in the trade 'cluster') is probably the most important case of cross-targeting (though, in principle, WTO rules set strict limits on their use) but the question is more general, as the range of potential instruments is large: conditions attached to financial assistance, whether provided bilaterally or by the IFIs; or to preferential trade access agreements (e.g. Lomé Convention, Generalized System of Preferences); withdrawal of other forms of cooperation (e.g. technology transfer); and comprehensive economic sanctions (e.g. embargoes, asset freezes, etc.), normally envisageable only as enforcement action under Chapter VII of the UN Charter ('action with respect to threat to the peace, breaches of the peace and acts of aggression').

Given the risks of misuse of these instruments, and consequent contagion effects from one policy area to another, it is essential to establish restrictive principles on their use, especially against non-participants. This might imply that:

- priority should be given to the use of enforcement mechanisms that are specific to the area under consideration and to the improvement of such mechanisms where they are inadequate;
- rewards to encourage compliance (e.g. trade and aid preferences) are often more appropriate than penalties (e.g. trade restrictions). Such 'positive' approaches, however, still leave open the problem of conflicting conditions imposed by different countries or group of countries. It would therefore be useful to clarify, at international level, an approach towards conditionality from an overall perspective of policy coherence;
- measures to secure compliance should respect the proportionality principle and should represent the least distortionary option;
- cross-targeting should be based on transparent processes and objective criteria supported, where possible, by impartial review mechanisms;
- action toward non-participants should require near-universal recognition of the need for such action, established through a

genuine multilateral process (i.e. open to all countries to which the action may apply).

3.2. INSTITUTIONAL APPROACHES TO DEALING WITH INTERACTIONS

Because of the increasing number and intensity of interactions between policy areas, improving the coherence of the system as a whole is an important goal. The 'cluster' work has shown that there is, more and more, a tension between the effectiveness issue (one problem, one instrument) and the coherence issue (each instrument should take account of its effects in other areas). Increased interdependence combines with more complex objectives to increase the importance of coherence. This is the challenge of complexity. Looked at in institutional terms, the requirements that arise from the 'clusters' are to:

- ensure that policy formulation in each functional area reflects the interest of the system as a whole, rather than the narrow mandate of a particular institution or ministers (e.g. macroeconomic policy cooperation taking greater account of adverse effects of interest and exchange rate instability);
- achieve consensus by making trade-offs across policy areas (e.g. higher LDC environmental standards in exchange for more aid and better trade access);
- resolve conflicts between mandates of individual institutions, including on new issues, which cut across the responsibilities of existing bodies (e.g. lead role on economic relations with Russia, negotiation of investment issues), and addressing negative interactions between policy areas (e.g. GATT trade liberalization, against desirability of environmental border taxes);
- more generally, the complexity of the interactions between policy areas raises the question of whether some form of

broad policy framework or orientations is desirable, within which the functional institutions could operate.

Currently, coherence is addressed by a combination of national governments acting within the organizations of which they are members, and cooperation between these institutions. Improving the effectiveness of these approaches must be the point of departure.

3.2.1. Cooperation between governments and between functional institutions

National governments clearly have a key role in ensuring coherence; this approach is currently the dominant one. However, the intensity of interactions identified above suggests that this approach is insufficient. Even if national governments coordinated perfectly internally, there is no forum to negotiate collectively. Representatives of Member States in different international bodies tend to see issues from the narrow perspective of their own institutional/departmental interest.

Increased cooperation between functional institutions is relatively undeveloped, and could fulfil at least some of the functions identified above. In particular, this may be a means of dealing with specific negative interactions, and avoiding duplication/inconsistency. However, there are intrinsic problems even in achieving these goals: membership and voting rules differ; each institution operates within its own mandate, which may constrain the extent to which they can take account of concerns in other policy areas; and the institutions are relatively weak, in the sense that they have little autonomy of action, and can only cooperate on the basis of consensus amongst their members, constraining the intensity and flexibility of cooperation.

Cooperation between IMF/World Bank and UN economic bodies on development issues is a good example. The 'cluster' (section 2.2) concludes that there is a need to reconcile short-term stabilization and structural adjustment with long-term developmental priorities. But both the mandate of and the power structure in the Bretton Woods institutions differ from those in the UN bodies. This makes effective cooperation difficult.

An intermediate question is the extent to which existing institutions could take on responsibility for increasing coherence in particular sets of policy areas. Possibilities include:

- *CSD*, whose purpose is to 'identify and agree upon long-term strategic goals for sustainable development' (G-7 Communiqué). However, CSD is an intra-UN body with limited status;
- *ECOSOC*, the senior UN economic body, which could play a role in improving internal UN coordination and providing a single UN interlocutor for IMF, World Bank and WTO;
- *the Development Committee of the World Bank and the Interim Committee of the IMF*. Both these bodies have broad membership, and treat some of the key policy areas identified in the clusters. There have been several efforts to use the Interim committee as a forum for looking at the full range of issues. There is also a current discussion of merging these two bodies. This could produce a body with an overview of financial, macroeconomic and development issues;
- *the WTO*, which might have the role of overseeing the rules of the game for international competition, as discussed in 'cluster' 1.

But these 'mini-coherence' bodies either can only deal with limited aspects of coherence, or have relatively low status. So, even if they are worthwhile, some important gaps will remain. Similarly, the G-7 is inappropriate for the role of providing overall coherence, given its lack of representativeness and resulting incapacity to provide credible guidelines for all participants and institutions.

3.2.2. How far to go in providing overall coherence?

There is much that can be done in improving cooperation between functional institutions. How far this should go, and, in particular, how far we should go in seeking institutional structures that can provide overall policy orientations, depends on a number of factors. The following considerations are relevant in making this assessment and in identifying factors to take into account in designing such a body:

- *there is a trade-off to be made between efficiency and dealing with complexity*. A body with very wide responsibilities for the international economic system would risk becoming only a talking shop because of the difficulty of identifying concrete issues for decision. The European Council provides an example of a more successful overarching body with a clearly defined role;
- *numbers*: with more and more emerging key players, any overarching body would need wider and wider membership, which, combined with a wide agenda, could make decision-making almost impossible. In the long-term, representation through regional constituencies could help here;
- *government failure*: it can be argued that in a rapidly changing world economy, efforts to address coherence issues could create more distortions than they solve, particularly if the combination of complexity and numbers makes decision-making slow. This concern has to be balanced against the strong arguments for action to deal with interactions that have been explored in this paper;
- *legitimacy and accountability*: current arrangements lack legitimacy in at least two respects: some functional institutions are not representative, and the body currently best suited to

taking a view of the system as a whole, the G–7, is a 'rich country club'. But creating an overarching structure with real influence itself poses important accountability problems, which need to be addressed.

3.2.3.   Some political challenges and a way forward

Managing interdependence raises important political challenges:

- issues of national sovereignty both for developed and developing countries;
- issues of leadership for the US and its partners within the G–7, and the tension between recognizing new players and retaining G–7 control;
- issues of democratic or non–democratic emerging powers (e.g. FSU, China, etc.).

These tensions show in the reluctance of many countries to engage in serious discussion of the long-term issues raised in this report. These tensions also mean that it is essential to adopt a progressive and pragmatic approach, building on what exists. This approach should involve:

- strengthening the weaker pillars of the system (environment, UN economico-social bodies, macroeconomic policy) in their own right, and to reduce asymmetries in decision-making;
- making more serious efforts to deal with key existing interfaces, focusing initially on the priorities identified in the specific issue-areas. This should involve greater coordination between existing institutions, and a bigger role for those existing institutions particularly apt to increasing coherence (CSD, IMF/WB Governing Committees, WTO, ECOSOC). This cooperation needs to be systematic, rather than *ad hoc*, and go beyond exchange of views, to

common analysis and common policy development on particular issues. It may sometimes require sharing the work of implementation and enforcement between institutions. It requires defining mandates and reducing overlap, while recognizing that some objectives can only be achieved by coordination. It may also require some strengthening in decision-making procedures within these institutions on the lines set out in the section on legitimacy and effectiveness. Better cooperation between Bretton Woods institutions and UN economic bodies is an obvious priority area;

- giving responsibility to particular institutions to coordinate some horizontal issues (e.g. World Bank Development Committee, CSD etc.) and considering *ad hoc* approaches to key problematic interactions which are not adequately dealt with by functional institutions (such as, perhaps, international crime);

- creating frameworks for coordination between multilateral institutions and national government (e.g. through development contracts);

- given that the G-7 will continue to play a role in some issues of coherence, links should be developed between the G-7 and key emerging countries and regional groupings, and improving the legitimacy of some of the existing institutions. The process for following up the institutional review itself will be an important precedent for linkages of this sort;

- increased involvement of regional groupings in policy-coordination and integration. This can help, both in reducing the number of participants in discussions, and by using regional links (APEC, EU links with Eastern Europe, North Africa) as means for wider discussion/consensus building. The degree of involvement of regional groupings in providing overall policy orientations should increase in parallel with the extent of their functional competencies and their development of efficient and legitimate structures;

- seeking to focus political interest on the question of whether a move towards a structure to enhance coherence is desirable and feasible. This will need consideration of both the intensity of interactions and the need for greater legitimacy in the management of the system as a whole.

In a long-term perspective, this progressive approach may provide the basis for a move towards an overarching structure with responsibility for providing a broad policy framework at international level.

Chapter 4

Key recommendations and conclusions

The work of the group has demonstrated that the current order is ill-prepared to cope with the three major challenges of the years ahead, i.e. the tensions created by increased economic interdependence, the emergence of new, powerful economic powers and the failure to integrate many developing countries into the world economy.

In shaping the new international economic order, policy-makers need to take into account the fact that many markets have become global and interactions between policy areas have intensified. This is reducing the scope for effective and autonomous national decision-making and increasing the importance of market failures at international level.

4.1. THE GOALS TO ACHIEVE

It is essential to focus on the goal of sustainable development, integrating economic efficiency, macroeconomic stability, social and environmental sustainability. For the European Union, this can be translated into more operational goals that the economic order should achieve:

- to prevent the resurgence of narrow-minded economic nationalism and the fragmentation of the world into competing blocs, which involves ensuring an adequate degree of stability at global level, and, in particular, macro-economic and financial stability, and allows genuinely global markets to operate effectively;

- to maintain and expand an overall liberal regime for worldwide trade and investment as a crucial basis for long term prosperity;
- to create the conditions for sustainable growth in developing countries. Europe has a major geopolitical interest in increasing the prosperity of its poorest neighbours.
- to ensure that economic activities in global matters are pursued in accordance with the objective of environmental sustainability and protecting the global commons.

4.2. THE KEY RECOMMENDATIONS

There is a need both to reinforce some pillars of the system, and to deal better with interactions between pillars. In terms of broad policy recommendations, related to the four main clusters of policy areas that have been considered, priorities are :

For 'new' and traditionally 'domestic' policy areas and their links to trade:

- *establish strong and effective international regimes*, not least in order to head off protectionist pressures. First priorities should include investment and competition. For invest-ment, it must be ensured that negotiations in the OECD are rapidly supplemented by a similar effort in the WTO. As regards competition, a plurilateral agreement among regulatory authorities might address some of the most pressing issues and pave the way for a global agreement that could be integrated into the WTO. In both areas, strong leadership from the European Union and, in particular, the

Commission in the years ahead will be crucial if these goals are to be met;

- *make the WTO one of the key pillars of the international economic order.* Its membership should become truly universal and its resources commensurate with its missions. It should develop criteria to help ensure compatibility between rules in new policy areas and the trade regime (notably in terms of criteria restricting use of trade policy instruments to enforce these new rules). An important step in this direction would be amending the GATT (Art. XX) to make WTO rules and Multilateral Environmental Agreements (MEAs) mutually compatible. Any linkage between trade and labour standards should be conditioned to consensus at ILO level on definition and monitoring of basic rights of people at work;

- *set up effective collaboration between the WTO, on the one hand, and the IFIs and the UN agencies, on the other.* This will help address the interactions between trade policy and other policy areas, while preserving the value of the WTO as a forum for facilitating and liberalizing trade.

For development and its links to other areas:

- *integrate more systematically the development dimension in all other policy areas*, notably trade and macroeconomic policy-making, to help remove barriers to the integration of developing countries into the international economy;

- *increase quality and, if possible, the volume of development assistance.* This requires focusing aid on human and social development, mobilizing private sector capital, continuing our debt relief efforts for the poorest countries, and promoting democratic and structural reforms;

- *improve donors' coordination and commitment from all the parties involved.* The introduction of 'development contracts' (also involving commitments, from the receiving countries' side, on the broader mechanism of domestic governance, including education and military, from the donors' side, on concessional aid, debt alleviation, market access) as well as the rationalization of the various UN economic organizations around a strengthened ECOSOC should be pressed forward;

- get the balance right between macroeconomic stabilization, structural adjustment and long-term development. This means better cooperation between Bretton Woods institutions and, more ambitiously, between them and the UN economic bodies.

For the environment and its links with development, trade and finance:

- *make UNEP the true environmental pillar of the international economic order.* It could become a 'World Environment Protection Organization'. This would involve the upgrading of the political representation of Member States in the governance of the organization, and the setting up of an integrated secretariat for the elaboration and the follow-up of global environmental agreements. Although regional environmental agreements are sometimes more appropriate, there is a need for such an international body to set minimum norms;

- *environment* is also one of the 'new' policy areas with important links to the liberal trade regime. As well as taking forward current work in the WTO, the relationship between WTO and a reinforced UNEP must be developed;

- *integrate more systematically the environmental dimension in all other policy areas.* Because of the powerful links between environmental protection and other policies, environmental commitments will not be met if all the necessary policy instruments are not mobilized. In particular, raising environmental standards in developing countries must be matched by better trade access and increased financial and technical assistance.

For finance and macroeconomics and its links to other areas:

- *achieve stronger cooperation/coordination of macroeconomic policies among the countries of the reserve currencies.* This requires agreement on objectives, and commitment to use policy instruments to achieve them. This is a crucial condition for reducing long-term misalignment of key currencies, adjustment asymmetries and the negative interaction between macroeconomic instability and trade liberalization. The completion of EMU, which would create a new powerful reserve currency, is a crucially important factor for achieving this goal;
- *set up better arrangements to help prevent crises* in particular countries, and to deal with them better if they occur. A strengthened surveillance mechanism under the auspices of the IMF was endorsed by the 1995 G-7 Summit at Halifax, and it is a good first step;
- *explore more systematic cooperation at international level between supervisors and regulators*, and assess the adequacy of supervisory standards in all international markets. The proposed G-7 led review will be important in this respect.

4.3. THE STRUCTURE TO STRIVE FOR

As regards the architecture of the economic order, we need to consider the functioning of the system as a whole, as well as its constituent parts, in a long-term perspective, while respecting the principle of global subsidiarity. This means that there is a need to:

- take account of more complex interdependencies while working with the grain of markets. This means emphasizing transparency, mutual recognition based on core standards, and market-based instruments (e.g. eco-taxes);
- enhance the legitimacy of institutions, and of the system as a

whole, while also increasing effectiveness/efficiency. Giving more players a say in decision-making must be accompanied by changes in decision-making arrangements that will increase effectiveness. This means associating the new economic powers and developing countries (greater rights and responsibilities) as closely as possible to the existing institutions and market-economy principles;

- ensure implementation of, and compliance with, agreed rules, notably through strengthening of dispute settlement mechanisms where they are weak or non-existent. Restrictive principles on cross-targeting and action toward non-participants should also be generalized. This should help to avoid recourse to unilateralism and contagion effects from one policy area to another.

Where there are no existing mechanisms for dealing with certain global issues, greater intergovernmental cooperation between key players could be a first step.

To improve the coherence of policies elaborated and implemented at the global level progressive and pragmatic approaches should be adopted:

- *governments should ensure coherence in their own policy positions* in different institutions. Furthermore, there is a need for coordination at all levels between different governments;
- *reinforcing the weaker pillars of the system* (environment, UN economico-social bodies, macroeconomic policy);
- *there should be increased cooperation between existing international institutions.* In practice, this would require greater clarity in the mandates of each of them, joint analysis and provisions for cooperation on the basis of clearly defined goals. This should, in due course, involve common positions or/and commitment to follow the same policy orientations;
- *regional groupings should be increasingly involved* in providing overall policy orientation, in parallel with the extent of their

functional competencies and their developing of efficient and legitimate structures;

- where simple inter-institutional cooperation is not enough, one institution should be entrusted with the responsibility for the specific interlinkages in question, even if this calls for a modification of its mandate (provided members of the overlapping organizations can agree).

Nevertheless, the existence of persistent and complex negative interactions between different policy areas suggests that reinforced cooperation may not be sufficient. Moreover, in order to have an adequate overview of the system and to ensure that policy formulation in each functional area is consistent with a broader policy framework, it could well prove necessary to envisage some sort of overarching structure. Such a structure would need to respect the principles of efficiency, democracy and subsidiarity.

The issue of how the coherence of the international system can be improved and whether some sort of overarching structure could have a useful role should be maintained on the agenda so these concerns can be assessed.

4.4. THE ROLE AND INTERESTS OF THE EUROPEAN UNION

The European Union is well placed to take a leading role in developing multilateral solutions to the problems of inter-dependence at global level, identified in this report; it also has a strong interest in advocating a multilateral rather than bilateral approach.

- It is well-placed because of its own successful experience of dealing with the integration process at the regional level, which has posed many of the same problems, albeit with different intensity, and with a strong political commitment to integration that is not present at global level. It is striking that the themes of efficiency and legitimacy, which are central to the future of the international order as described here, have also been identified as guiding principles in the Commission reflection paper for preparation of the IGC.

In addition, the key interactions dealt with in this report relate mainly to the external dimension of the first pillar of the Union — trade, development, environment and (with EMU) macroeconomic policy. So there are areas where the Union needs to participate effectively in international negotiations;

- It has a strong interest, in addition to the persuasive arguments that multilateral solutions are more beneficial for all participants, because the relative lack of EU political integration reduces the effectiveness of a bilateral approach *vis-à-vis* US and/or Japan.

This has implications for the role of the Commission:

- the Commission should play a leading role in increasing coherence at the Union level in the areas forming part of the first pillar. This is a prerequisite for achieving coherence at global level. But it must be recognized that many aspects of these issues will remain national responsibilities (e.g. economic policy under EMU). The Union will need to look at how to act coherently in areas of mixed competence, and in dealing with interactions between policy areas. This is an issue for the IGC starting in 1996 (procedures for ensuring the European Union speaks with a single voice), but also in dealing with specific interactions (e.g. between IMF and WTO);
- the Commission also has an important role in demonstrating that European solutions to specific problems of interdependence can provide models for global solutions. The single market process is the most important source of such lessons.

Similarly, the Commission's long-term perspective on European integration allows it to take a long-term perspective on global developments, which provides a useful addition to the more short-term, nationalistic position adopted by other participants.

There are two more key issues for the European Union:

- The EU has a strong interest in maintaining and developing a positive approach to regionalism. In many areas regional solutions make sense because the problem is essentially regional in nature; they can reflect greater regional interdependence, or provide a partial solution to a global problem. In addition, regional solutions can form the basis for global solutions, by identifying workable approaches. The global architecture needs to take better account of the development of regional groupings, not only in relation to matters of trade or regional security, but also as a means of reconciling the need for global policy coherence with the diversity of values and models of society. However, it has to be ensured that regional developments remain compatible with multilateralism. This poses a hard question of the balance of EU interests: should the European Union seek maximum freedom of manoeuvre for its own regional development, or ensure that multilateral initiatives and rules are given priority? Given the European Union's traditional commitment to multilateralism and the broader risks to Europe if other so-called regional groupings (APEC, ASEAN, NAFTA, MERCOSUR) were to pursue inward-looking strategies, the case for the EU to support effective multilateral disciplines seems strong;
- it makes senses for the EU to support a transfer of power away from the industrialized group of which it forms a part, in favour of emerging economies. The European Union should support a bigger role for emerging players, because its

101

objectives for the economic order cannot be achieved without involving them.

The Forward Studies Unit

The Forward Studies[1] Unit was set up in 1989 as a department of the European Commission reporting direct to the President.

It consists of a multicultural, multidisciplinary team of some 15 staff who are responsible for monitoring the forward march of European integration while identifying structural trends and long-term prospects.

The Commission decision setting the Unit up[2] gave it three tasks:

- to monitor and evaluate European integration to 1992 and beyond;
- to establish permanent relations with national bodies involved in forecasting;
- to work in specific briefs.

The Forward Studies Unit has, to date, produced wide-ranging reports on new issues which, as a result, have frequently found their way into the mainstream of the Commission's work, developing a house style which applies a research method designed to bring out the diversity of Europe (Shaping Factors, Shaping Actors), developing an all-round and/or long-term view which makes it easier to secure consensus above and beyond particular national interests, keeping a watching brief on and an ear open to movement in Europe's societies by setting up links with research and forward studies institutions, and holding regular seminars on specific themes which are attended by prominent figures from the arts, the cultural sphere and universities and representatives of civil society, together with the President or a Member of the European Commission.

The futurological function has gradually developed outside the Unit, within several of the Commission's Directorates-General which are keen to adopt a strategic approach. The Unit serves as a point where all the various future-oriented think-tanks inside the Commission can meet.

For some years now, the need for a forecasting function having grown as the work of the European Union has become wider and more complex, the work programme for the Forward Studies Unit has been updated each year so that it can be reoriented to meet specific needs and towards maximum cooperation with all the Commission departments concerned.

Information about the Unit's current work is put out in the quarterly *Lettre des Carrefours* and on an Internet site.

Notes

1 European Commisison, Forward Studies Unit, ARCH-25, Rue de la Loi 200, B-1049 Brussels, tel. + 32-2-295-6735, fax +32-2-295-2305, Internet http://europa.eu.int
2 Minutes of the 955th meeting of the European Commission, 8 March 1989.

Other titles published in this series

The Future of North–South Relations

The Mediterranean Society: A Challenge for Islam, Judaism and Christianity

Shaping Actors, Shaping Factors in Russia's Future